CW01023408

A GUIDE TO

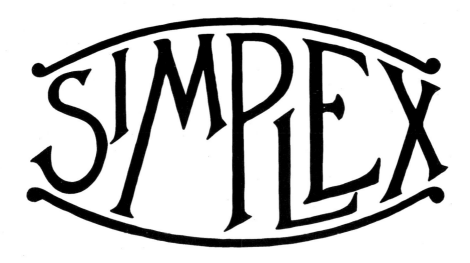

NARROW GAUGE LOCOMOTIVES
(INCLUDING LIST OF EXISTING LOCOS IN ENGLAND, SCOTLAND & WALES)

D. R. HALL & J. A. S. ROWLANDS

SAPIENTIA NON VI

Published by The Moseley Railway Trust

First published 2001 by The Moseley Railway Trust.

ISBN 0-9540878-0-1 (Softbound)
ISBN 0-9540878-2-8 (Hardbound)

Printed by Postprint, Taverner House, Harling Road, East Harling, Norwich, NR16 2QR.
email: postprint@plateway.co.uk

Acknowledgements

In producing this book we have referred to source material held by Bedford Archive Service, Alan Keef Ltd. and the Narrow Gauge Railway Society.

We are grateful to the following people who have given information and assistance:

Vincent Bailey, Peter Cross, Bob Darvill, Peter Excell, Eric Fresne, Chris Kisch, Alan and Patrick Keef, Sydney Leleux, Andrew Neale, John Palmer, Rob Pearman, John Pease, Ken Scanes, Mike Spall, Marcus Trollope, Clive Walters, Robin Waywell, Huw Williams, Andrew Wilson, Pete Wood.

Unless stated, all photographs are original Motor Rail material, loaned by Alan Keef Ltd., Bob Darvill and Pete Wood, and are reproduced by kind permission of Alan Keef Ltd.

All profits from the sale of this book will go to the **Moseley Railway Trust**, a volunteer run organisation dedicated to preserving industrial narrow gauge locomotives, rolling stock and other associated equipment.

E-mail: davehall@rustons.fsnet.co.uk
E-mail: jrowlands@acm.org
Website: www.mrt.org.uk/simplex

Contents

This book is dedicated to the
memory of our friend Peter Cross,
Simplex enthusiast within the
company for 44 years.

Preface

In preparing this guide to Simplex locomotives, we have deliberately restricted our objectives in a number of ways. We have specifically confined ourselves to narrow gauge locomotives, describing each type manufactured by the company with photographs where possible so that the general enthusiast has enough information to identify a particular member of the Simplex species. We also list existing locomotives in England, Scotland and Wales in a similar fashion to the companion publication "A Guide to Ruston Narrow Gauge Locomotives." We do not cover standard gauge locomotive types, nor tramcars, nor railcars. Neither do we attempt to provide the complete company history or a works list.

The reason for deciding to restrict the scope of the book in this way was primarily to ensure our task was *achievable* within a reasonable period of time. We are working under the maxim that it is better to publish a relatively cohesive part of the story than to publish nothing at all. There is so much to the Simplex story that a small booklet could never do it justice, but equally there is no substantive work available or close to publication that we know of on the subject. We have felt increasingly frustrated by this omission in the documentation of industrial locomotive history, even more so because we know that a number of our fellow enthusiasts have stated their intention to produce the definitive book. Hopefully, by publishing this guide we will encourage some of the experts in the field, many of whom have kindly assisted in compiling it, to take the next steps towards the comprehensive Simplex book. The authors would of course be happy to offer their services in this regard.

In this vein, we also invite readers to provide corrections or additions, where known. There are certain types of early locomotive, such as the Fowler engined types, about which very little is known and no photographs have come to light. Any information that you can provide would be gratefully received. Although we have done our utmost to ensure accuracy, it is inevitable that the occasional error has crept in and we would welcome amendments for inclusion in any future edition.

The works number series has been obtained from the Motor Rail order books held by the Bedford Archive Service and, where possible, has been cross-checked against the Motor Rail records held by Alan Keef Ltd. Where there are small gaps in a batch, such as the 20/28 H.P. type, this may be due to the loco not being built, the record sheet being missing, the order being cancelled or, on rare occasions, the number being allocated to another product, for example a dumper. Where at least one set of records shows a loco, we have included it. Where neither set records a particular number, we have omitted it.

Weights are given in British Long Tons unless otherwise stated.

The authors hope you enjoy reading our book and trust that you will find it as interesting to read as it has been to compile.

D.H. & J.R., August 2001

The following abbreviations are used in this book:

AK	Alan Keef
AKL	Alan Keef Ltd.
B.H.P.	Brake Horsepower
B&F	Burnholme & Forder Ltd.
cm	Centimetres
cu	Cubic
cwt	Hundredweight
Dsm	Dismantled
ECL	E.C.Lenning (Proprietary) Ltd.
ft	Feet
H.P.	Horsepower
in	Inches
INCO	International Nickel Company
km	Kilometres
lbs	Pounds
Lt.	Light
Ltd.	Limited
mm	Millimetres
M.P.H.	Miles Per Hour
MR	Motor Rail Ltd.
MRSP	Motor Rail Simplex (Proprietary) Ltd.
MRTC	Motor Rail and Tramcar Company Ltd.
M&R	Margolis and Ralph Engineering (Proprietary) Ltd.
nr.	Near
Pty.	Proprietary
Rly.	Railway
RMP	Railway, Mine and Plantation Equipment Ltd.
R.P.M.	Revolutions per Minute
SMH	Simplex Mechanical Handling Ltd.
S/O	Steam Outline
U.K.	United Kingdom
W.D.L.R.	War Department Light Railways
w/n	Works Number
yd	Yards

Notes:

1 Short Ton = 2000 lb = 907 Kg
1 Long Ton = 2240 lb = 1016 Kg

A Brief Company History

For 77 years The Motor Rail and Tramcar Company Ltd. (MRTC) and its successors produced a highly innovative and successful range of tramcars and small internal combustion locomotives, thousands of which were sold in the U.K. and in many other parts of the world.

The Early Development

The company founder, John Abbott, had interests in the East India Tramways Company, who were operating horse trams. In 1907 experimental work began on a scheme to motorise these trams using petrol engines combined with mechanical and later electrical transmission. This resulted in a patent application (British Patent No. 18314/09) in 1909 by John Abbott's son, John (Jack) Dixon Abbott, for the "Simplex" gearbox. This simple yet rugged design utilised three parallel gear shafts, providing forward and reverse gears in two speeds.

The Motor Rail & Tramcar Co. Ltd. was formed in 1911 and the first meeting of the directors, Mr. John Abbott (chairman) and accountant Mr. George Gale, took place at the registered office at 79 Lombard St., London. At this meeting George Gale was appointed company secretary at a salary of £100 per annum. John Abbott took one thousand shares in the new company, with George Gale taking one hundred. The intention of the new company was to manufacture and sell railcars and tramcars utilising petrol engines and the Simplex gearbox. The first vehicles were built at the Phoenix Ironworks at Lewes, Sussex. The arrangements for the use of these works cannot have been ideal because by 1914 the company was looking for new premises and several enquiries were made and sites visited. However, at a board meeting of October 1914 it was agreed that in view of the uncertainty of matters generally created by the war, the idea of a new works

An early MRTC tramcar supplied to the East India Tramways Co. Ltd.

was to be abandoned for the present. However, the matter became urgent in 1916 after a meeting with the consulting engineers of the War Office, Messrs. Rendall, Palmer & Tritton. The War Office required "Petrol Trench Tractors" of 600-mm gauge that were capable of drawing 10 to 15 Tons at 5 miles per hour and the MRTC tendered for and was successful in gaining a contract to build the Tractors.

John Abbott had visited Germany in about 1911 and was alarmed at the stockpiles of light railway equipment for army use, including internal combustion locomotives. Worried that there was no British equivalent for use on temporary military supply railways, he set about designing such a machine. The first tractor was produced in 1915. John's sons, Tom Dixon Abbott and John Dixon Abbott were also involved in the design of the so-called Simplex Tractor, and indeed they jointly submitted a patent application for the Tractor (No. 127399) in 1918.

Early in 1916 the MRTC entered into an agreement with the Bedford Engineering Company to use its premises at Houghton Road, Bedford and by May of that year had also opened its own office at 33 Houghton Road. John Abbott died on the 23rd of August 1916 and his eldest son, John Dixon Abbott was elected to the office of Chairman. The younger son, Tom Dixon Abbott had joined the board only a month before the death of his father. John remained as Chairman until 1957 and Tom would be actively involved until 1963.

Most of the workforce at Bedford was shared between locomotive and crane manufacture and the first Simplex Tractor produced at Bedford took 3 months to produce, but by the end of the year they could produce 20-25 per week using a workforce of less than 20. Tractors could be produced at this rate primarily due to the subcontracting of major parts manufacture. All major parts except the frame were bought in and final assembly took place at Bedford Engineering. Deliveries continued through 1917 and 1918, with over 700 tractors of 20 Horsepower and 40 Horsepower types delivered in 1918. At the start of 1918, a new site was purchased in Bedford, this being a former laundry in Elstow Road. Later that year, it was also possible to purchase further land at the front of the works, including the access road, and land at the rear including a rear access point. The company office moved to 16 Elstow Road in January. The first full batch of locos to be produced at the new works comprised works number 1642 onwards.

The following year John Dixon Abbott resigned from his post of General Manager, becoming Consulting Engineer to the company, a post that he retained during all his remaining years as Chairman. The post of General Manager was subsequently shared between Tom Dixon Abbott and a new appointee to the board, Alexander Harris-Brown.

With the cessation of hostilities in France, a considerable quantity of light rail equipment, including Simplex Tractors, became available as War surplus, initially at Purfleet and later in France. Many of these were acquired by industrial concerns eager to exploit this modern form of traction. MRTC, although interested in purchasing the Purfleet locos to sell on, could not afford to buy a large quantity. Tom Dixon Abbott eventually bought a number with the offer for the company to purchase them from him as required. Many ex War Department Simplex Tractors also passed through the hands of dealers. One such was William Jones Ltd., with whom the company later bought 66 derelict Tractors from a site in France under a "pooling" arrangement, whereby each firm would overhaul half the Tractors and share the profit. Sales of pooled Tractors occurred from 1922 to 1929, when the pooling arrangement was cancelled.

The Locomotive Hire Business

In 1921, after enquiries from several customers, the first discussions over locomotive hiring took place. Hiring could be an attractive proposition for customers interested in assessing the new form of traction. Tom Dixon Abbott favoured the idea, but the company was not in a position to proceed for financial reasons.

A Dorman 2DWD diesel powered front-control Motor Rail dumper of 3 cu yd capacity and 1950s vintage. The engine, clutch radiator and fuel tank are all identical to Simplex locos of the period.

Instead, a hire business was set up as a separate concern, under the control of the Abbotts, and favourable purchase prices and credit terms were agreed. This business would in 1924 become Petrol Loco Hirers Ltd., and in turn this company, including its 103 locos, would be acquired by MRTC in 1930 for £12,400. As a result of the increase in locomotives being powered by diesel units, the company also decided to set up Diesel Loco Hirers Ltd. as a joint stock company with Petrol Loco Hirers Ltd., and this was done in 1935. In 1960, the name of Petrol Loco Hirers was changed as it was effectively defunct with no petrol locos having been built since 1941. The name change to Dumpahirers Ltd. in 1960 reflected the hire of another of the company's products – the diesel dumper.

Works Expansion

In 1920, the adjoining Grosvenor works of Slogger Engineering became available and was purchased. This completed the purchases of land and buildings, apart from the purchase of adjacent cottages on Elstow Rd. and Grosvenor St. that Tom Dixon Abbott would arrange to acquire as and when they became available and would rent out to company employees. In c1921 the two factory buildings were joined together by an arched roof, making one large building. The original laundry would have two stories added on stilts due to the inability of the existing structure to support the additional floors. An office block was built in 1938 on the front of the laundry, and in 1952 a completely new building was erected at the rear of the premises for the production of 9 Ton locos.

Product Developments

The first standard gauge locomotive was produced in 1919. Tramcars and railcars continued to be produced, but standard and narrow gauge locomotive manufacture dominated in the 1920s. The first discussions about diesel locos took place in about 1928. The directors appreciated the benefits of the new form of power unit

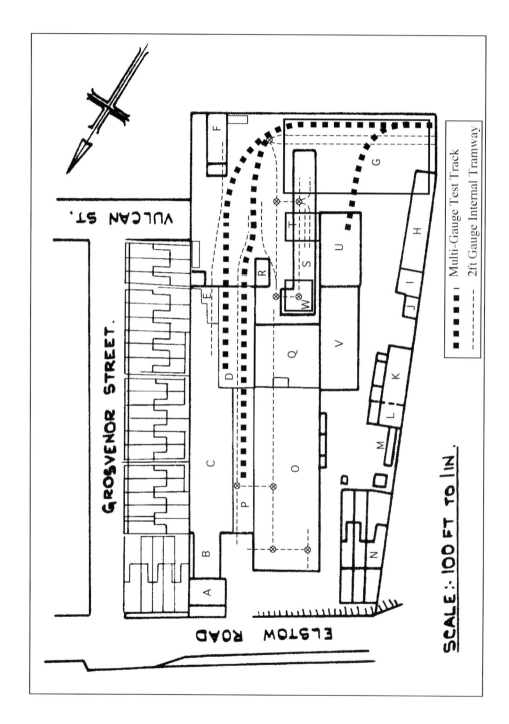

Site plan of the Simplex Works at Elstow Road, showing all major buildings.

| | Multi-Gauge Test Track |
| | 2ft Gauge Internal Tramway |

SCALE :- 100 FT TO 1 IN.

Key to Site Plan

A   New office block erected in 1938.

B   Original offices of Simplex Works.

C   The original Simplex Works building, a former Laundry. Used initially for locomotive assembly, then later for gearbox, clutch and cab manufacture. In approximately 1952 this single storey building was extended to three floors. The ground floor eventually became a parts store and the rear became packing and then goods inwards. There was a chimney towards the rear which was demolished in 1928.

D   Extension built in c1926. It became an erecting bay by 1967 and by 1974 was in use as a packing area.

E   1920 extension to the original Simplex Works.

F   Pre-1926 building which was originally a paint store but was refurbished prior to 1967, then let to Matisa as a store. It was demolished between 1971 and 1974, after which the area was used as a steel store.

G   New assembly building for fork truck attachments erected between 1971 and 1974. In the 80s it was let out to the local authority education department as a store.

H   Garages built in the 1920s or 1930s. By 1974 they were in use as storage for wheels, axles and patterns. They were partially demolished to free space for building G.

I   Early stores dating back to before 1919.

J   Extension to Stores, added prior to 1941, demolished by 1972 and this area used for Managers' car parking.

K   Formerly Gowers' Works in 1919, before this part of the site was acquired by Motor Rail. Later used as a garage until converted into the works canteen in 1955. By 1986 it was in use as offices.

L   Extension to Gowers' Works in 1919. In use as a store shed for bright bar for Premac by 1974.

M   Cycle sheds.

N   Houses. Demolished by 1972 and this area was then used as a car park.

O   Original Slogger Engineering Company Works, acquired in 1920. Latterly used for the machining and sheet metalwork shops. The front part of this building was let out to Caslake Ltd. in the 1970s.

P   Originally a cartway between Simplex and Slogger works. This was arched over in c1921 to become the heavy erecting bay for locomotive assembly. It was equipped with a travelling crane. It was still in use for loco assembly in 1974.

Q   Extension built in 1934.

R   Post-1926 boiler house. The roof accommodated a cast iron rain water storage tank. It was demolished between 1967 and 1971.

S   Built between 1926 and 1934. Demolished in 1966. This consisted of a variety of structures. The top end contained the "plonker" where hardening was carried out. Lower down the "letter store" accommodated obsolete records.

T   Erected post-1966 as a crane bay, this building was in use as a paint shop by 1971.

U   "High Bay" for erection of 9 ton locos. Built in 1952 and fitted with 15 ton travelling crane, by 1966 it was divided into welding booths and areas for general fabrication.

V   Built during the Second World War for manufacture of parts (probably tank gearboxes) for the War Office. Later used as a stores building, it became an area for welding and cutting by 1966 and welding booths by 1972

W   Temporary wooden storage building erected in approximately 1972. Purpose unknown.

and were investigating the offerings of various suppliers, including Lister, Ailsa Craig, McLaren, MAN and Dorman. Although some early locos used other types, by far the most successful was the Dorman 2HW (later 2DW and 2DWD). In a shrewd business move, Motor Rail negotiated an exclusive licence to use this engine in their locomotives. This proved particularly important when competitors started trying to make pirate copies of Simplex locos. Diesel conversion kits were also supplied to existing petrol loco customers, allowing the economy benefits of a diesel to be realised in the early bent frame Tractors. The production of diesel locos once again boosted demand and the production numbers that had settled down to about 100 per year after the war started to rise again in the mid thirties. The War Department also placed orders in the Second World War, generally for the 20/28 B.H.P. type, although this time the locos were mainly used in Army depots and the like. Many of these locos remained in store until the end of the War, once again being sold into industry as war surplus. Once again, a number of these were bought back for "reconstruction," although in practice this could amount to little more than a fresh coat of paint.

In 1939, the company introduced a completely new product, the Motor Rail Dumper. This utilised the same Dorman twin cylinder engine and clutch arrangement as the locos, together with a similar Dixon Abbott gearbox. Dumpers were also made available for hire.

A Change of Name

In 1931, the directors decided to change the name of the company from Motor Rail & Tram Car Co. Ltd. to Motor Rail Ltd. The name was officially changed by the Registrar of Companies and certified as such on 16th April 1931. George Gale, the surviving company founder, died in January 1942. He had been company secretary since the establishment of the firm in 1911. Joint general manager Alexander Harris-Brown resigned in 1945 on the grounds of ill health, leaving Tom Dixon Abbott in sole charge.

Export Market

After the war, although the British market was still very much active, it became clear that the future of the company depended on the expanding export market, particularly in Africa. With a small company such as Motor Rail Ltd., it would be infeasible to set up a large number of overseas offices and it was therefore necessary to recruit agents in the countries where there would be most demand. Motor Rail did this very successfully, setting up exclusive marketing deals with companies such as Parry & Co. for India, Paterson, Simon & Ewart for the Far East, Wigglesworth & Co. Ltd. for East Africa (including Tanzania, Kenya, Mozambique and Uganda), and E. C. Lenning Proprietary Ltd. for South Africa, Rhodesia and some of West Africa. Railway, Mine and Plantation Equipment Ltd. (RMP) were responsible for most of the rest of the world, including West Africa. Such was the size of the market in South Africa that prior to 1953, E. C. Lenning had sold over 500 Simplex locos in this region.

Ernest Lenning and his wife Dagmar were good friends of Tom Dixon Abbott, and the sales of the Simplex locos and spares in South Africa boomed in the late forties and early fifties. When Motor Rail floated 25% of the company on the stockmarket, Ernest Lenning's confidence in the product was such that he sought to acquire some shares himself. Lennings could sell as many Simplexes as they could get; they never had a single loco in stock. The supply of locos was limited due to the unavailability of raw materials in the U.K. in the post war years. In 1951 this factor and the lack of availability of a flameproofed Simplex design threatened to damage sales prospects. For instance, in 1951 Lennings already had enquiries for 24 of the 32/42 B.H.P. locos for delivery in 1952, yet their share of the 1952 production would only be 15. Added to this, major competitors such as Ruston and Hornsby were aggressively attempting to enter the market and for the first time Lennings found themselves beaten on price by the flameproofed Ruston machines. Ruston now had available the LBU locomotive with its short and narrow frame, ideally suited to underground working, which was being advertised intensively in South Africa and marketed by Hubert Davies.

The issue of flameproofing did not sit easily at Bedford. First of all, Tom Dixon Abbott's objective was to keep the Simplex design simple, such that it was cheap, reliable and easily maintainable. Added to that there were difficulties in avoiding Ruston's patents. These factors combined to make Motor Rail slow to respond to the threat. After the death of Ernest Lenning in October 1951, his step-brother Rudi Martin, whom he had groomed as his successor, was put in charge. Rudi suggested setting up some sort of manufacturing operation for Motor Rail locos and spares in South Africa. There was even a suggestion of a collaboration with RMP, Orenstein & Koppel and Allens in a manufacturing venture. It was not until 1953 that Lennings were authorised to make certain spares in country under licence to avoid the lack of supplies affecting customers.

The South Africans and New Locomotive Developments

In late 1953, Dagmar Lenning, as the sole shareholder in E. C. Lenning, resolved to sell the majority of her holdings and Motor Rail investigated the option of purchasing these. Unfortunately Mrs. Lenning had received a favourable offer, which Motor Rail did not feel they could match. Thus it was that control of Lennings passed on to a consortium of three businessmen: John Davidson, an accountant, Benny Tessel of Sodium Chemicals (Pty.) Ltd. and his brother, Mr. P. Tessel. Motor Rail were concerned about the sale and the way Lennings were doing business. Firstly, Lennings appeared to be charging their customers a high price for spares, and this was encouraging other companies to produce "pirate" spares for supply to the mines. Secondly, Motor Rail were concerned that Lennings might be producing parts other than those authorised. Certainly at least one loco frame had been manufactured. As a result of these concerns the Motor Rail board decided in April 1954 to establish a South African company, Motor Rail (Simplex) Proprietary Ltd. (MRSP), to control the supply of spares produced or purchased in South Africa. The company recruited Neville Still to look after the company on site. He was sent out in June 1954, being met at the airport by Lennings people, but he never did acquire the level of information and control that Motor Rail were seeking. Lennings continued to encourage Motor Rail to consider some sort of manufacturing operation in country. The political situation was such that sanctions might be imposed on imported goods that could be manufactured locally, and conversely government support was available for the setting up of new businesses.

Although loco deliveries improved in 1954, they again dropped in late 1955, partly due to problems at Bedford with the introduction of all-welded loco frames. By 1957 loco deliveries from Bedford had risen to 6 locos per month and would continue to rise to 10 per month in 1958, but the spares supply situation under MRSP was worse than previously under Lennings. Added to this, another threat was emerging from competitors The Hunslet Engine Company Ltd., in the form of locos with hydraulic transmission. Again, Tom Dixon Abbott was reluctant to adopt this new form of transmission, the relatively unsuccessful "Simtran" transmission not being ready for delivery until 1960. However, that did not stop another South African firm, Margolis and Ralph Engineering (Pty.) Ltd. (M&R), from experimenting with torque converters in Simplex locos. M&R were also producing their own loco designs and starting to make pirate Simplex locos. Lennings would later acquire M&R, but it turned out that M&R was not the only company they had their eyes on.

So concerned were Motor Rail at the situation with respect to supply and pirating of spares and locomotives that in May 1959 they terminated the exclusive marketing agreement with Lennings, an act which would lead to an acrimonious legal battle between the two companies. Lennings served a summons on MRSP in December 1959 claiming a sum of £318,504 in damages as a result of the cancelled agreement.

The situation would drag on until 1963 only to be resolved in the boardroom at Bedford when it emerged that the Lennings directors had purchased sufficient Motor Rail stock to exert pressure for change at the management level. Tom Dixon Abbott withdrew completely from the management team, leaving Tom

Beighton in charge. It seemed he could not face standing by and watching the company being run by outsiders. By 1965, the Lennings people were in a position to launch a full takeover bid, acting through an Irish registered company, Loco Holdings Ltd. It was at this point that the remaining Abbotts, including Tom's son, John R. Abbott, sold their shares and resigned from the board. However, John R. Abbott remained on the management team.

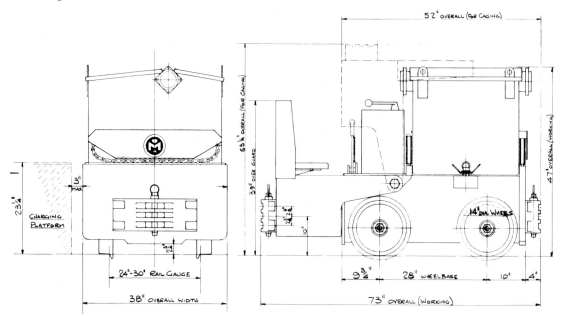

Proposed 2½-Ton battery-electric locomotive. Although some patterns were made, no prototype was ever completed.

The changes at Bedford happened swiftly. Virtually the first items to appear on the agenda were the issues of flameproofing, hydraulic transmission and narrow locos for mines. Tom Beighton was removed as works manager in 1966 and replaced by Tony Wenham, a former RMP man appointed by Benny Tessel, who was the majority shareholder. Although designs for a battery electric locomotive had been produced, and a new prototype hydrostatic loco was available in 1966 (the 40H), Lennings were now successfully producing locos to the M&R design, and at least one was diverted to Bedford on its way to Shalee Silver Mines in Ireland. This loco formed the basis of the design for the new U-Series hydrokinetic loco, the first of which was despatched in 1966 to fulfil an order from the International Nickel Company (INCO) of Canada. The U-Series would go on to win for Motor Rail the Queen's Award for Industry in 1969 at a time when 90% of the company's output went for export. Nearly 200 U-Series locos were produced, even though the export markets were shrinking rapidly. The U-Series would be enhanced with a hydrostatic version in 1967. In a departure from previous Motor Rail policy, different engine variants were offered, including Deutz, Ruston and Dorman, however after the first deliveries to INCO with Deutz engines in 1969, the sales team was encouraged to market this as the preferred engine.

However, Mr. Wenham also presided over a reduction in staff at Bedford and the sale of the freehold of the Simplex Works and the various properties that Tom Dixon Abbott had bought over the years. He also sought to diversify the business by buying designs and subcontract work in. The first acquisition was The Low Loading Trailer Co. Ltd., followed by fork lift attachment manufacturing work for Oldham and Sons Ltd. This part of Oldham's business would be taken over in 1970. The design for a concrete breaking machine, the "Thumper" was acquired, and manufacturing work for road sweeping machines was also undertaken.

On the locomotive side, a larger version of the U-Series, the T-Series, was developed in 1972, as was the smaller G-Series with mechanical transmission in 1968 and the H-Series for underground work in the same year. Locomotives built to the original Simplex layout continued to be produced as the S-Series. RMP continued to be active in marketing these and they had Motor Rail hold stocks of standard 40S and 60S locos for quick delivery to RMP customers.

Simplex Mechanical Handling

In 1972, with the new designs established, the South Africans disposed of their interest in the company to the Luton-Based Burnholme and Forder Ltd. (B&F). They brought with them a number of other companies and the resultant reorganisation left Motor Rail Ltd. as a holding company for a group of general engineering companies, including the new Simplex Mechanical Handling Ltd. (SMH), which was responsible for all operations related to locomotives, dumpers, trailers and fork lift attachments. Thus SMH became part of the Motor Rail Group of Companies, with Mr. Wenham still in charge. The financial situation during this period reflected the depressed state of the U.K. economy. Suppliers were feeling the pinch too, and Motor Rail's long-term collaborators, W. H. Dorman of Stafford, withdrew their extended credit terms soon after the B&F takeover.

The new arrangements only lasted until 1977, when B&F went into compulsory liquidation. At this point a new financial backer, Mr. Andrew Wemyss stepped in. Wemyss was a Scottish businessman who owned brick factories in Scotland, tea plantations in Kenya, sheep farms in Australia and hotels and vineyards in France. His Wemyss Development Company bought control of SMH and Motor Rail Ltd. and Tony Wenham remained in charge until 1984. Although he remained a director, he died shortly afterwards. Martin Everitt took over as general manager in January 1985 but by this time the locomotive business had reduced to a very small part of the company's operations.

Alan Keef

In 1986, with a one-off locomotive order received, SMH subcontracted the manufacture of a locomotive for the first time in its history, to Alan Keef Ltd. (AKL), a small light railway engineering firm operating from Cote in Oxfordshire. One further order would be completed in the same way over the next year until finally in August 1987 the decision was made to cease locomotive manufacture and close the factory at Bedford. All equipment and machine tools were sold at auction at Elstow Road on 15th September. The locomotive business was transferred to AKL at its new premises near Ross-on-Wye, with the attachment spares business being transferred to a new company, Simplex Attachment Spares Ltd. SMH continued to deal in drum handling machinery but the original 1911 Motor Rail company was dissolved on 15th December, 1987.

AKL continues to provide spares for Simplex locos and even new locomotives if required, although under the Alan Keef name. The last Simplex was produced in 1992, a 60S of the same general layout as John Abbott's original Petrol Tractor design. Simplex locos can still be found working in British and overseas industry today, and indeed the oldest loco in British industrial service is believed to be Motor Rail 5402 of 1932, still at work on a Scottish peat farm.

The Works and its People

Perhaps one of the most remarkable things about Motor Rail was their size in comparison with their obvious competitors. In the 50s when the company was probably at its peak, there were no more than 150 employees, 120 of whom were involved in production, the remainder in the offices. In contrast, Hunslet had many hundreds of employees and Rustons had a **workforce of** thousands to call upon, albeit in a much more diverse range of products. Nevertheless Motor Rail, this tiny company, through the brilliant simplicity of its design, the quality of its manufacture and its network of worldwide agents was able to compete very successfully against the bigger players. As with other small family firms, employees recall the friendly atmosphere at Simplex Works with a great affection, which perhaps would not have existed in a larger undertaking. These sentiments are delightfully summed up in the words of former employee, Peter Cross:

> "In my early days they took me down into the works and said 'this is Bill Millard, he builds gearboxes and he's been here 25 years,' then we went further down and they said 'here's somebody else, he's been here 30 years,' then someone else who'd been there 40 years. I couldn't believe it. I hadn't been on the Earth that long. I've often smiled that I was there 44 years. It was that sort of place. You didn't move, it was too good."

A view of the main erecting bay in the late 1970s. 60S, 40S and 101T-Series locos are evident.

The Layout of the Motor Rail Simplex Locomotive

This diagram below shows the layout of a plate-frame 20/28 H.P. loco, but the general layout is similar on all the company's "Simplex" designs and originated with the 20 H.P. Petrol Tractors built for the War Department Light Railways. This loco is a left hand drive, i.e. the seat is arranged so that the gear levers are operated by the driver's left hand. In some models, the seat was positioned on the opposite end of the loco, thus becoming right hand drive. The reasons for different models having either left or right hand drive are not known with any certainty, although it is likely that in the earlier models the arrangement was dictated by the position of the speed control lever on the engine.

The transversely mounted engine and gearbox can be seen along with the chain final drive to the wheels. The standard wheels were made of chilled cast iron, a material that is very hard wearing but, when it finally does wear, is virtually impossible to machine, as many owners of preserved locos have found to their cost.

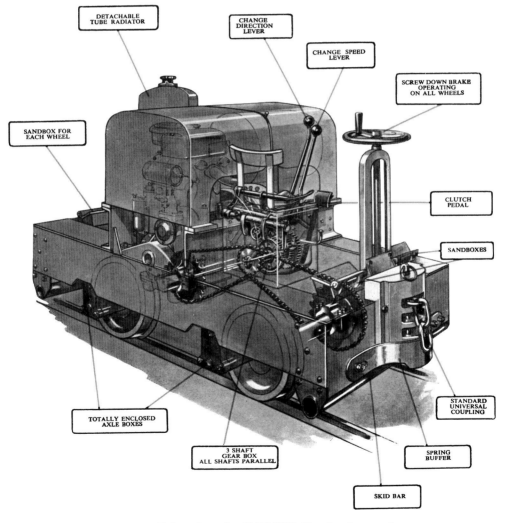

"Phantom" drawing of a 20/28 H.P. Simplex locomotive

Detachable Tube Radiator

All but the very early radiators on Simplex locos were of the Davies Patent type and were arranged so that tubes could be replaced or repaired individually. This is something that is quite an advantage over other types such as Rustons, where the whole radiator had to be replaced and a fairly major strip down was needed to get at the radiator.

Change Direction Lever

As its name implies, this operated the forward/reverse feature of the gearbox.

Change Speed Lever

This lever selected the gear ratio. Normally only two speeds were available, but on the larger models such as the 32/42 H.P. and 60S there was a third gear. There was no synchromesh on the gearbox, as on motorcars of the time, and "double de-clutching" was required when changing down a gear.

Clutch Pedal

Early locos employed an inverted cone clutch, an unfortunate characteristic of which was a tendency to stick when worn. This was replaced in later models by a flat clutch plate, with the 48/63 H.P. locos having a double clutch plate. The foot-operated clutch pedal was a disadvantage on systems where many turnouts had to be negotiated as the driver was constantly climbing on and off the loco. The loco could not be driven whilst walking alongside.

Sandboxes

Four of these were fitted, one for each wheel and they were operated by foot pedals.

Brakes

These operated on all four wheels by use of a brake wheel and screw. Cast iron brake blocks were provided. Originally a handwheel was provided for applying the brakes. In some later locos a lever was provided, this being much easier and quicker to apply in an emergency.

Axleboxes

These employed gun-metal bearings and were lubricated by sprung oil pads. Leaf suspension springs were used.

Standard Universal Coupling & Spring Buffer

This was first introduced in 1920 with loco 2014. It was a solid casting and usually had three slots for different coupling heights but some had five such as the straight-framed 20 H.P. petrol locos. A spring buffer was fitted to clear the coupling and this provided some shock absorption between the loco and its load.

Skid bar

This was provided to stop the wheels from sinking too far into the ground in the event of a derailment. It was made from tubular steel but was not all that strong and many extant locos show the signs of derailment – a bent skid bar.

Optional Fittings.

As optional extras steel tyred wheels, whistles, cooling water circulating pumps and electric lighting and starting could be provided. Cabs could also be fitted, which came in several variations, the most obvious being the roof – curved or pointed. Cabs could also be retrofitted to locos purchased without a cab; these being obvious by the engine cover design. Engine covers designed for cabbed locos are supplied with the cab side missing. Tropical-type cabs and full length canopies could also be fitted.

The bare frame of a welded frame 20/28 H.P. loco seen from below. The slots in the central plate on the left hand side are for the linkages from the brake column. It is on the top of this plate that the works number can be found stamped on locos built after c1936. When ex-War Department locos came for reconstruction and their works plate was missing and their number unknown, a new number would be allocated and this can be found be stamped on the left hand side of the rear engine bearer. Works plates on most locos can be found on top of the rear (left on this picture) engine bearing cross-member. Some petrol locos, 20/26 H.P. for example had the works plate on the plate between the front sand boxes due to the engine timing retard/advance lever being mounted in the place usually taken by the works plate.

The Dixon-Abbott gearbox initially provided two speeds in each direction, with later versions providing three speeds for the heavier locomotives. Each gearbox comprised three parallel shafts, the Simplex layout negating the need for right-angle bevel gears. The input shaft was driven direct from the engine, and the output shaft carried the duplex drive sprocket for the driving chains to the wheels. Each shaft ran in roller bearings with the speed selection gears being in constant mesh. The different speeds were engaged using sliding dogs on the output shaft, whereas the direction selection was effected using a sliding primary gear on the input shaft.

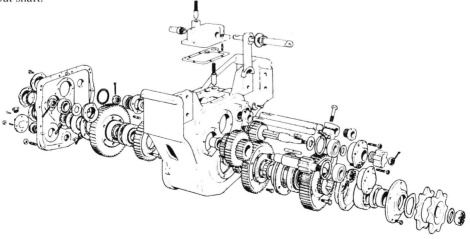

Exploded diagram of a three speed Dixon-Abbott gearbox as fitted to 60S loco.

A 1918 Motor Rail & Tramcar Co. Ltd. brass works plate from a 20 H.P. loco. This quotes the address of the registered office in Lombard St., London.

A 1935 worksplate from a 12/20 H.P. loco. Although a number of variations are known to exist, the majority of plates in the Motor Rail Ltd. era are similar to this one. During the Second World War cast iron plates were temporarily introduced as a substitute for the usual brass.

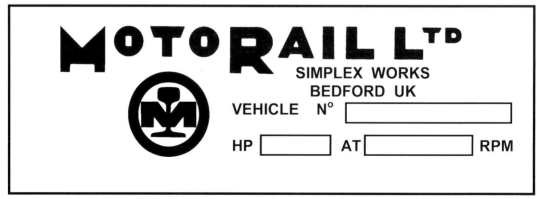

Aluminium plates were later introduced incorporating the new Motor Rail logo and, after 1969, the logo for the Queen's award for industry.

DUMPERS

3 Cu. Yard. FRONT AND REAR CONTROL

LOCOMOTIVES

2 TO 15 TONS

SIMPLICITY.	Designed for operation by unskilled labour.
ACCESSIBILITY.	Direct access to all Working Parts cuts Maintenance Costs to a minimum.
ECONOMY.	Diesel operation ensures Maximum Economy.
STABILITY.	Assured by Low Centre of Gravity and Perfect Weight Distribution.
RELIABILITY.	Guaranteed by experience gained in the manufacture of this type of Equipment over a quarter of a Century.

● *All the above Important Features are backed by an EFFICIENT SPARES and SERVICE DEPARTMENT ensuring prompt and careful attention to all orders for Spare Parts.*

Write for Full Particulars—

MOTOR RAIL LTD

SIMPLEX WORKS - BEDFORD
ENGLAND

Codes :

Telegrams :	A.B.C Engineering, 6th Edition	Telephone :
SIMPLEX, BEDFORD	and Bentleys	BEDFORD 4521

Section I - Petrol Locomotives

20 H.P.

The 20 H.P. loco or "Petrol Tractor" was Motor Rail's first loco type and is commonly known as "Bow", "Boat" or "Bent" framed, although at Motor Rail they were only ever known as "Bent" frame. The type was by no means the first internal combustion loco but was probably the first successful mass produced type. It made its mark in the First World War, when hundreds were constructed for the War Department Light Railways to operate the 2-ft (60-cm) gauge lines that were built to supply the trenches.

MRTC had tendered for the War Office contract in January 1916 after John Dixon Abbott had met the consulting engineers to the War Office, Messrs. Rendall, Palmer & Tritton. The specification was for "Petrol Trench Tractors" of 600-mm gauge, weight not exceeding 1 Ton per axle and to be capable of drawing 10 to 15 Tons at 5 miles per hour. The resulting design incorporated features that were to form the basis of Motor Rail designs for half a century such as the transversely mounted engine, driving position and the Dixon-Abbott patent gearbox.

A standard 2½-Ton 20 H.P. Simplex Petrol Tractor.

After the war, cheap war-surplus Petrol Tractors started to open up new markets for narrow gauge railway haulage where steam locomotives were thought too heavy or just too expensive to buy and run. *The Quarry* of June 1919 featured an article regarding the 20 H.P. "Simplex" petrol or paraffin locomotive, which pointed out the inherent advantages of the internal combustion engine such as comparatively low first cost and economy in running. It also mentioned the flexibility of the "motor engine" as regards varying speeds and loads. Part of this read: "It is coupled to a heavy flywheel and inverted cone type clutch, which in turn is directly coupled with the 'Dixon-Abbott' patent spur wheel gearbox. The combination ensures steady running and no jar when running and hauling various loads from 1 to 12 miles per hour. This makes for less wear and tear than is experienced with a steam engine of similar capacity".

The 2JO petrol engine manufactured by W. H. Dorman & Co. Ltd. of Stafford powered the 20 H.P. loco and this choice of manufacturer was to stay with Motor Rail on and off for over fifty years.

After the war a 4-Ton version became available and this used the same engine, running gear and specification as the 2½-Ton but had a straight channel frame, although it retained many features of the "bent" frame construction. Straight-framed locos were available as 2½-Ton versions but only if the gauge was greater than 2-ft.

Optional fittings were available on post-war locos such as a short canopy for the driver that was fitted with tarpaulins that could be rolled down against inclement weather so as to leave a small rectangular hole for the driver to see fore and aft. A full cab of wooden construction was also available.

An old-style 4-Ton, 20 H.P. straight channel framed loco – note the 5-slot coupler.

In 1929, a new frame type was introduced on the 20 H.P. locos, which also formed the basis for other classes that were being developed, including the 20/35 H.P. petrol, the 25/40 H.P. petrol, the 12/16 H.P. diesel, the 16/24 (58xx series) and the 20 H.P. diesel. This new frame was 7-ft 11-in long and 4-ft 10-in wide (on 1-ft

In the early 30s Motor Rail began to produce kits so that diesel engines could be retro-fitted to 20 H.P. petrol locos by them or in the customer's own workshops. The engines were those used in the 20/28 H.P. locos, beginning with the 2HW Dorman-Ricardo type.

10-in to 2-ft 8½-in gauge locos) and was of a much simpler construction than those used previously. 20 H.P. locos using this frame began at w/n 5001 and finished at w/n 5094. In 1930 such a loco would have cost £190.0s.0d new.

Number Series (built between 1916 and 1932)

New Locos
200-379, 842-1116, 1162-1255, 1290, 1291, 1387, 1388, 1642-1854, 1856-1859, 1892-1911, 1932-1941, 1980-2020, 2041, 2045-2060, 2075-2091, 2093-2097, 2099-2119, 2135, 2147-2150, 2152-2157, 2171, 2172, 2260, 2287-2291, 3660, 3661, 3686-3688, 3695, 3703, 3708-3712, 3715-3719, 3722-3725, 3733, 3734, 3738, 3739, 3741-3746, 3748, 3749, 3751-3774, 3792, 3832, 3833, 3838, 3851, 3883, 3971, 3972, 3978, 3991, 3993, 4001, 4006-4086, 4155, 4159-4161, 4165-4167, 4170, 4179-4183, 4199, 4203, 4214, 4501-4552, 4556-4562, 4564-4575, 4576, 4578-4580, 4587-4622.

Note 1: 1290 & 1291 were post-war built locos but these numbers had also been given to 40 H.P. locos built for the Ministry of Munitions.
Note 2: w/n 200 is the earliest recorded loco, however it is believed that this was not the first. It is possible that earlier locos used engines other than Dorman, possibly by White & Poppe.

New Numbers Given to "Reconstructed" or Overhauled Locos
Note that not all locos given new numbers were rebuilds ("reconstructed"). Sometimes a loco that was in to be re-engined or overhauled for its owners was renumbered when no trace of its original identity could be found.

2175, 2179-2214, 2216, 2217, 2292, 3650-3654, 3657, 3681-3685, 3689-3694, 3696-3700, 3704, 3705, 3713, 3714, 3720, 3721, 3727-3729, 3735-3737, 3775, 3778-3781, 3787-3791, 3794-3796, 3807-3811, 3823, 3824, 3828-3831, 3834, 3835, 3837, 3841, 3844, 3845, 3849, 3850, 3852, 3854, 3855, 3857, 3858, 3860-3879, 3881-3894, 3960-3963, 3969, 3970, 3974-3977, 3981-3990, 3992, 3994-3999, 4002-4005, 4575, 4577, 4625.

New locos built to new frame design
5001-5094.

4-Ton 20 H.P. locos hauling sugar cane at Cairns, Australia.

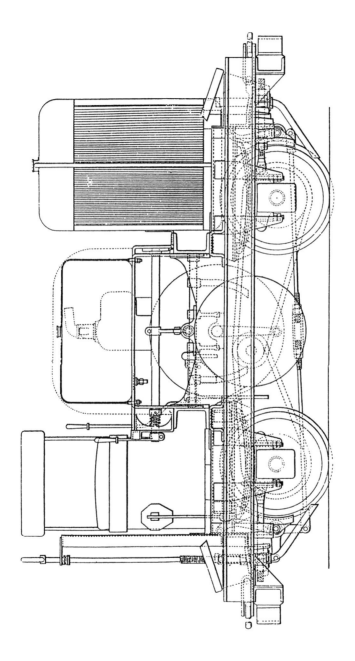

Side Elevation of an early prototype 20 H.P. Tractor taken from the 1918 patent application. A number of differences are evident in the production models when compared with this prototype. These include a shorter wheelbase, addition of cast iron ballast weights, improved driver's seat and the use of a wheel rather than a lever for the screw brake control. Scale 1:16

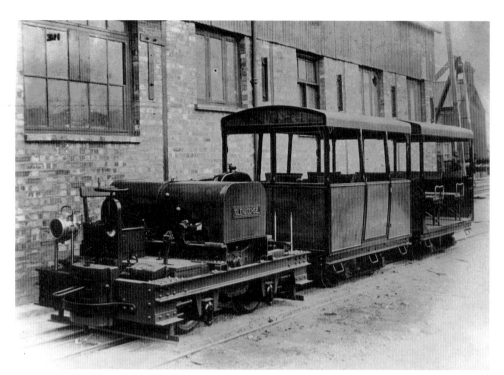

"GLENLOCHSIE," w/n 2086, supplied to Sir Archy Birkmyre Bart in 1921. This 2½-Ton 2-ft 6-in gauge loco was provided complete with coaches and is pictured on the cartway outside the laundry prior to the construction of the erecting shop.

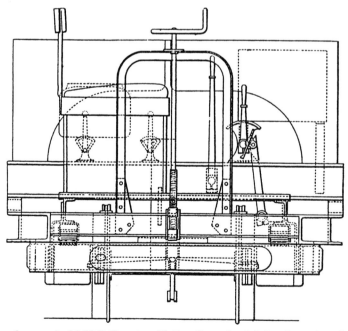

Rear elevation of an early 20 H.P. Tractor. Notice the raised driver's seat and the wide support bracket for the brake column, both tell-tale signs of very early 20 H.P. locos. Scale 1:16

40 H.P.

The 40 H.P. types were built for the Ministry of Munitions alongside the 20 H.P. for use by the War Department Light Railways in the First World War and they were built with varying degrees of protection for the driver to protect him from shrapnel and sniper's bullets.

The three variants were the "open," the "protected" and the "armoured." The "open" had just the end plates of armour plate and a canopy on height-adjustable pillars for protection, whereas the "protected" had this plus side doors and visors. The "armoured" on the other hand was completely enclosed with an armour-plated roof, which curved down at each end and had slits for the driver to look through – rather like a tank. It is reported that a .303-in calibre bullet shot at 50 yards range would make only a small dent in the armour.

The power unit of these locos was the Dorman 4JO petrol engine, coupled to the two-speed Dixon-Abbott gearbox.

Many of the later-build W.D.L.R. locos never made it to France and were auctioned off after the war to various concerns that required cheap motive power. Also many locos, both unused and those returning from France, were "reconstructed" by Motor Rail and Wm. Jones under their pooling arrangement. Reconstructed locos varied in appearance from completely original to having new bodywork in the form of cast ends in place of the armour plate. Such locos were still listed in the 1932 Motor Rail catalogue but were designated "40/50 B.H.P.," although no such designation was used in the order books, all being shown as 40 H.P. Two narrow gauge varieties were available, the 6-Ton (gauges 60-cm to 1-Metre) and the 8-Ton (gauges 2-ft 6-in to 3-ft 6-in). The 6-Ton used the old W.D.L.R.-style of loco frames whereas the 8-Ton used a new type of

An "open" loco.

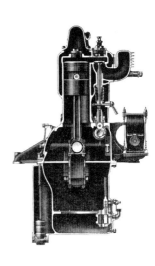

Cross-section of a Dorman 4JO engine.

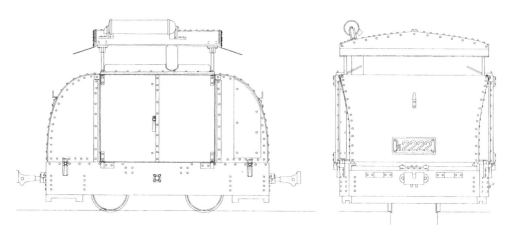

Drawing of a W.D.L.R. "protected" 40 H.P. loco. Scale 1:48 (Courtesy of Eric Fresne)

frame. Ex-W.D.L.R. locos were also reconstructed to standard gauge by Motor Rail and other companies such as Kent Construction. These locos varied from being a standard narrow gauge loco with new axles and **a** buffing block bolted across the armour plate ends to brand new frames and proper running gear with the correct buffer height.

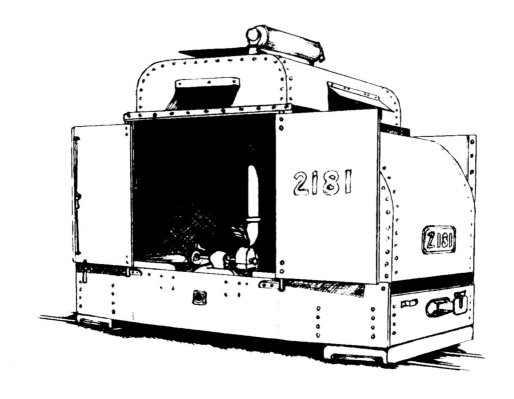

An "armoured" 40 H.P. loco pictured with doors open. (© Vincent G. Bailey)

Number Series (Narrow gauge locos only)

Built between 1917 and 1918 (Ministry of Munitions original locos)
Built between 1919 and circa 1930 (reconstructed and other new locos)

New Locos.
380-603, 1280-1386, 1952-1959, 2061-2074, 2120-2123, 2127, 2130, 2133, 2134, 2136, 2137, 2139, 2257-2259, 2261, 3655, 3656, 3706, 3707, 3813-3818, 3826, 3827, 3964, 4162-4164, 4168, 4185-4198, 4200-4202, 4209-4213, 4215, 4216.

Note 1: 480-489 are duplicated in the order books with different W.D.L.R. numbers, destinations and delivery dates.
Note 2: 1290 & 1291 were also numbers given to 20 H.P. locos.
Note 3: 3965 was a 6-Ton, 3-ft gauge loco and had the same appearance as a 40 or 40/50 H.P. loco but was actually supplied without an engine so that it could be fitted with a customer-provided Fowler diesel engine (H.P. unspecified).

Reconstructed Locos. (Narrow gauge locos only)
2176, 2177, 2230, 2231, 2233, 3658, 3659, 3662-3680, 3701, 3702, 3726, 3747, 3776, 3784, 3797, 3803, 3812, 3819, 3839, 3840, 3842, 3843, 3846-3848, 3853, 3856.

A post-war 6-ton, 40 B.H.P. loco at work on the "Chilean Nitrate Pampas." Note the new cast ends and new type of canopy.

It was resolved that the freehold of the piece of land at the front of the company's premises over which the deeds only give the company right of way, be purchased from Mr. Ray for the gift of two pedestals and vases at £1 agreed.

Company Minute Book 21-6-1918

An 8-ton "40/50 B.H.P." loco – note the new frame.

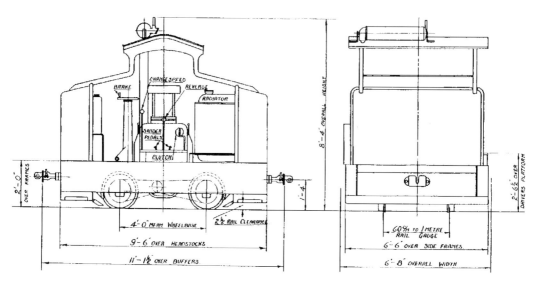

Drawing of a 6-ton "40/50 B.H.P." loco as per the 1932 catalogue. It is assumed that this frame design (the original War Department Light Railways type) was also used on new-build locos after World War 1. Scale 1:48

10/20 H.P. and 12/20 H.P.

The 10/20 H.P. was the first new narrow gauge petrol loco design since World War I and was one of Motor Rail's lightest and lowest powered models, with a weight of only 2 tons. Fewer than 30 of these locos were built between 1929 and 1940, making it also one of Motor Rail's rarer locos, although remarkably four survive in the U.K. Dorman engines powered the majority – either the 4MVB or 4MVR, both of which were initially rated at 10/20 H.P., the latter being uprated later to 12/20 H.P. However, the last 4 built had the Austin 12/4 engine of 12/20 H.P. fitted. The Dorman engines do not seem to have been a success, as spares such as big-end bearings were ordered within a month of one loco being delivered. Some locos had their engines rebuilt several times in less than 5 years and one had a replacement engine within 4 months. Dorman-engined locos can be distinguished from later models due to the silencer being placed closer to the centre of the loco on the gearbox side of the radiator.

This series of locos incorporated a new design of gearbox and clutch. The clutch comprised a single dry plate which was totally enclosed within the engine flywheel. The new gearbox design was smaller and lighter, employing ball and roller bearings throughout. The output drive sprocket was also moved forwards, making it equidistant from the front and rear axles. The lever positions for first and second gear selection were also reversed in the new arrangement. All these features became the standard for subsequent types.

Number Series (built between 1929 and 1940)

      6001-6024, 6031-6032, 6035-6036.

      Note 1: 6032 was a rebuild of 6019.
      Note 2: 6016 was a rebuild of 6008.
      Note 3: Parts of 6020 were used in the construction of 6031 and 6035.

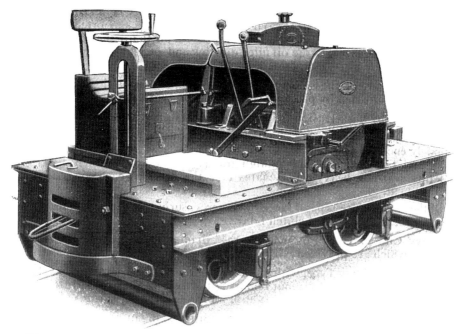

Photograph of a Dorman-powered 10/20 H.P. taken from a 1930 catalogue.

Note 4: 6012 was returned to Bedford in 1937 for an Austin 12/20 H.P. engine to be fitted.

Note 5: 6009 was the first loco to be designated 12/20 H.P.

Note 6: The number 6036 was allocated to George W. Bungey, possibly for an unidentified rebuild.

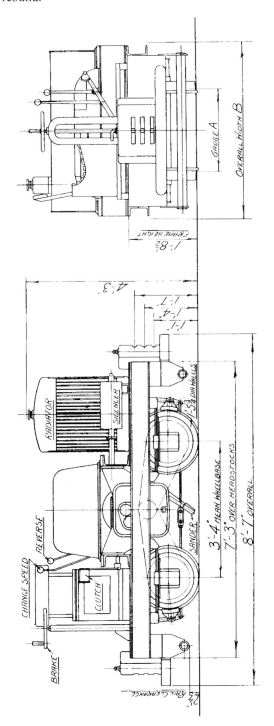

Drawing of a Dorman powered 10/20 H.P. loco. Scale 1:28

GAUGE A 1'-6" to 1'-10" OVERALL WIDTH B = 4'-7"
GAUGE A 1'-10" to 2'-0" OVERALL WIDTH B = 4'-3"
GAUGE A 2'-0" to 3'-0" OVERALL WIDTH B = 4'-8"
GAUGE A 3'-0" to 3'-6" OVERALL WIDTH B = 5'-2"

20/35 H.P.

The 20/35 H.P. type was first introduced with w/n 5201, which was a 4-Ton model ordered by Contractor's Plant Ltd. and despatched on 28th July 1930 to J. Makin Ltd. Sand & Ballast Pits, Great West Road, Hounslow, Middlesex.

The 20/35 used the new style of straight channel frame that was introduced on the last batch of 2JO engined 20 H.P. locos in 1929. The engine used was Dorman's 4-cylinder 4MRX petrol engine, with cylinders of 80-mm bore and 130-mm stroke. This was the first locomotive type to use right-hand drive. In other words, the gear levers were operated by the driver's right hand, a mirror image of the layout of earlier locos. It appears that the layout was dictated by the position of the carburettor on the engine, it being simpler to place the throttle control on the carburettor side.

Number Series (built between 1930 and 1937)

      5201-5421, 5451-5459, 5461.

      Note 1: 5413 was a rebuild of 5329.

w/n 5260 preserved at the Abbey Pumping Station, Leicester.

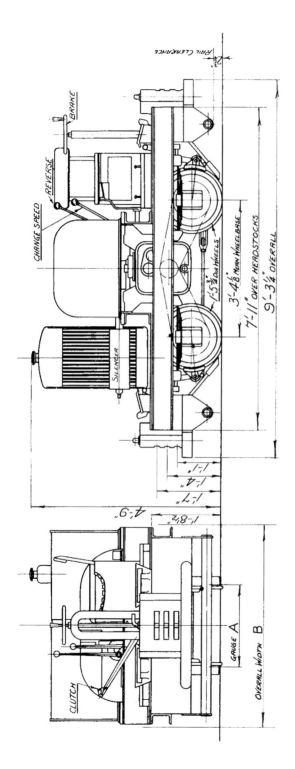

GAUGE A 1-8" TO 1-11½"	OVERALL WIDTH B = 5-2"	
GAUGE A 1-11⅝", 2-8½"	OVERALL WIDTH B = 4-10"	
GAUGE A 2-8⅝", 3-6"	OVERALL WIDTH B = 5-3"	

20/35 H.P. loco. Note the offset radiator and large exhaust silencer. Scale 1:28

25/40 H.P. (Ford Engined Loco)

Only one of these 2¼ -Ton petrol-engined locos was built in 1932. It is listed in the order book as 25 H.P. and was despatched to the Ford Motor Co. at Dagenham on 2nd March 1932 for display. It was later returned and spent time on hire at several sites. The type was listed in the 1932 catalogue (as 25/40 H.P.) but no picture or further information was provided. The loco is assumed to have been fitted with a Ford AA 4-cylinder, 3-Litre side valve engine, the industrial version of the Ford A. The frame was the same type as used on the 20/35 H.P. locos.

Motor Rail records indicate that 20/35 H.P. loco w/n 5461 of 1937 was "built up" from loco 7001. It was fitted with an engine that had previously been fitted to 20/35 H.P. loco 5250 of 1931. Presumably the new engine was fitted to the overhauled 7001 and the whole lot sold as a new loco. The customer was Dinmor Quarries Ltd. and the loco was despatched to Llanfair P.G. station, Anglesey on 31st March 1937.

<u>Number series</u> (built 1932)

7001.

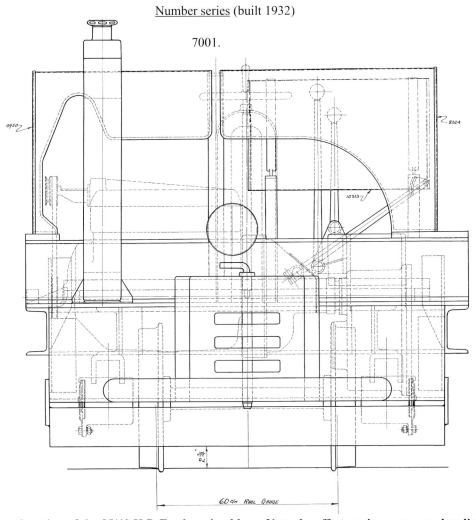

Front elevation of the 25/40 H.P. Ford-engined loco. Note the offset engine covers and radiator designed to deal with the extreme position of the fan belt drive pulley. Scale 1:12

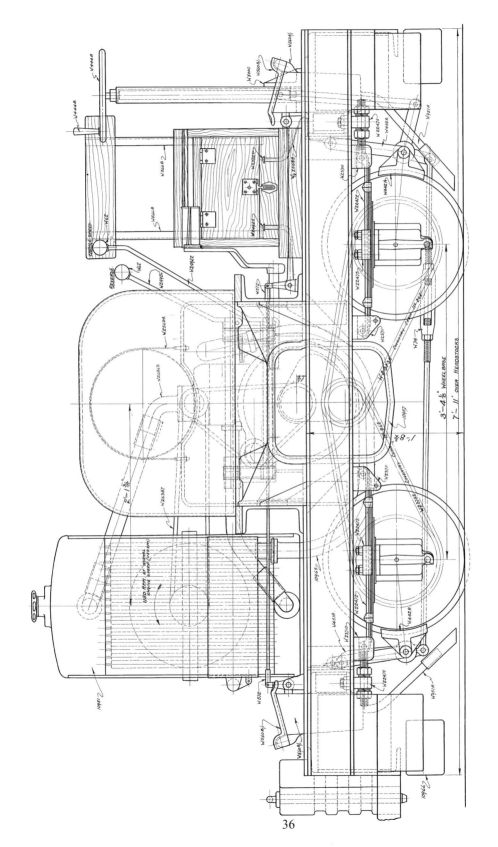

Side elevation of the Ford-engined loco. The frame is similar in all respects to its contemporaries except for the extra ballast weights needed to bring the loco up to the standard weight of 2½-Tons. Scale 1:12

20/26 H.P.

The 20/26 H.P. is one of the models commonly known as the "plate frame type" due to its frame being made from steel plate as opposed to the channel section of most of the older models. It was available as 2½ and 3½-ton variants.

The 20/26 H.P. type was fitted with the Dorman 2JOR petrol engine, similar to the engine fitted to earlier 20 H.P. types. In contrast to the 2JO, the 2JOR had a detachable "Ricardo" cylinder head. Many of these plate-framed locos were actually listed as 20 H.P. in works records but all are referred to here as 20/26 H.P. to avoid confusion.

One easy way to tell a 20/26 H.P. apart from the very similar looking plate framed 20/28 H.P. diesel is the exhaust. On a 20/26 H.P. this ends in a large silencer next to the radiator, whereas on a diesel loco it usually ends just under the engine cover on the opposite side and has an exhaust operated whistle on the end. The petrol locos had the whistle screwed directly into the cylinder head and this worked off the engine compression. Of course, many 20/26 H.P. locos were rebuilt with diesel engines later in their lives, both by their owners and MR, thus effectively making them 20/28s. These rebuilds have the tell-tale sign of a hole in the front cross member where the radiator outlet pipe formerly passed through to the engine. The 20/28s built new did not have this feature.

20/26 H.P. w/n 7033. Macclesfield Borough Council purchased this loco new at a cost of £275 in 1936 for use on construction of the London Road housing development. It remains in the Council's ownership and is now part of the Moseley Railway Trust collection. (John Rowlands)

Number Series (built between 1934 and 1941)

4701-4728, 4801-4815, 7021-7023, 7025-7098, 9101-9104.

Note: The following locos are known to have been reconditioned by MR in 1952. They were fitted with Dorman 2DWD diesel engines, given new works numbers, and sold as new 20/28 H.P. locos:

Old Number	New Number
7032	9539
7080-7081	9540-9541
7083-7087	9660-9664

20/26 H.P. loco w/n 4701, re-engined with a diesel and seen here in April 1961 as Arnold's No. 19 on a Double Arches to Stonehenge sand train on the Leighton Buzzard Light Railway. At Leighton Buzzard, the standard 2¼-Ton Simplex models could often be found with ballast weights from bent frame locos fitted in place of the normal skid bars. (S. Leleux)

His Worshipful the Mayor,
Said how proud he had been,
To hear the works in Elstow Rd.
Had been honoured by the Queen.
Amidst all these proud persons
Let no one cast a veil,
The toast was made by one and all
To the health of Motor Rail.

Extract from poem written to mark the receipt of the Queen's Award for Industry on 30th May, 1969.

The award is presented by the Lord Lieutenant of Bedfordshire to Tony Wenham (right).

(Courtesy of Bedfordshire Times and Citizen)

Section II - Diesel Locomotives

McLaren Engined Locos

The first diesel locos, 5501 and 5502, were to have been fitted with Helios diesel engines of 18 H.P. made by J. & H. McLaren Ltd. of the Midland Engine Works, Leeds. In fact the Motor Rail records show that the pair were not built due to problems with the engines and the McLaren-Benz 30 H.P. diesel engine was substituted starting with loco 5503, which was delivered in 1929. The loco was available in weights ranging from 4 to 5 Tons. The majority of this type were exported and most were fitted with foot-operated brakes. The cost of a diesel loco at that time was £578.0s.0d, which was around double the cost of the equivalent petrol engined loco. Locos from 5517 to 5520 are known to have been fitted with the MR2 McLaren-Ricardo engine, whereas locos from 5531 were "equipped with latest MDB2 engine." This latter engine had a bore size of 135-mm and a 200-mm stroke. It incorporated a Benz pre-chamber and had a nominal running speed of 800 R.P.M.

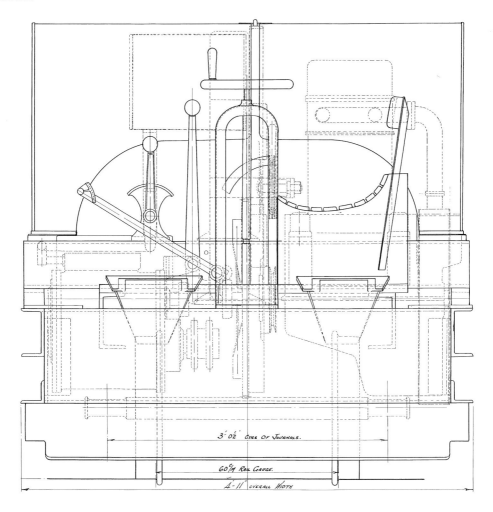

The drawing above is believed to be of a 30 H.P. loco and is dated 1929. It will be noted that it has the old style channel frame as used on the early 20 H.P. petrol locos. Scale 1:12

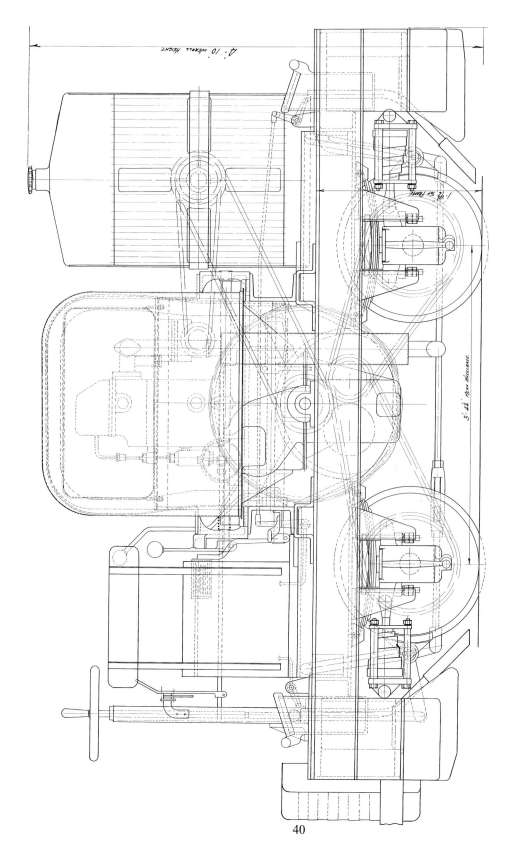

Side elevation of 4-Ton diesel (assumed 30 H.P McLaren). Note the right-hand drive layout and old type frame and gearbox. The engine governor control is mounted on the brake column. Scale 1:12

This drawing shows the later plate frame version of the McLaren engined locomotive as illustrated in a contemporary McLaren catalogue.

<u>30 H.P. Number Series</u> (built between 1929 and 1936)
5503-5509, 5512, 5514-20, 5522-25, 5531-5533

<u>10 H.P. Number Series</u> (built 1930)
5513   3½-Ton

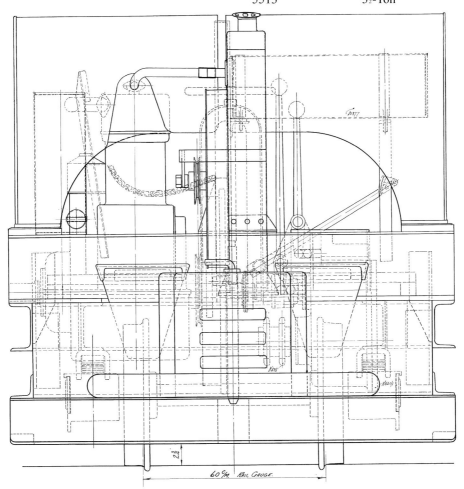

60 %m. RAIL GAUGE.

Front elevation of 10 H.P. McLaren engined loco. Scale 1:12

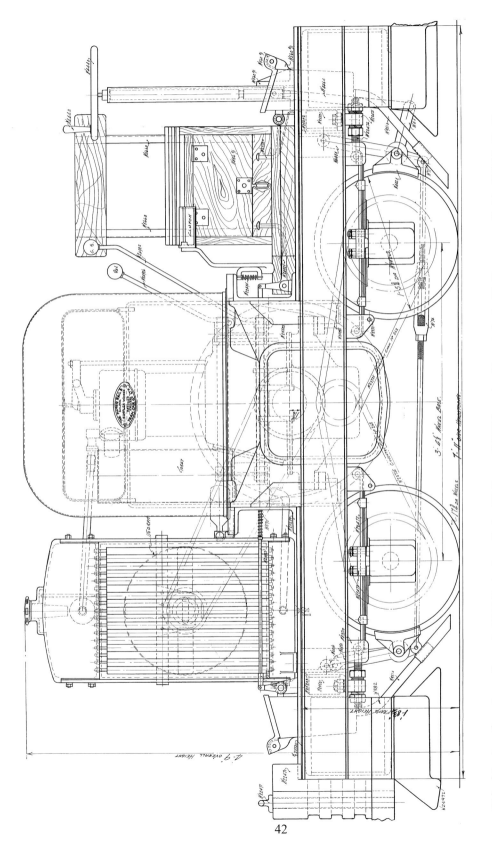

This side elevation shows the only 10 H.P. single cylinder McLaren BR118 engined loco to be built. It was supplied in 1930 to the Penmaenmawr & Welsh Granite Co. Ltd. for use at their Trefor Quarry. It was subsequently re-engined with a Dorman 2HW in 1934, only 4 years after delivery. As can be seen, this loco uses the same type of channel frame as the 20/35 H.P. loco. Scale 1:12

20 H.P.

The 20 H.P. diesel was introduced in 1930 and was fitted with the Dorman 2RB engine, producing 21 B.H.P. at 800 R.P.M., 26.5 B.H.P. at 1000 R.P.M. and 36 B.H.P. at 1500 R.P.M.

The designation was changed to 20/36 H.P. in 1932 and this was used until 1934 when the 2RB engined locos became known as 25/36 H.P., although some ex Petrol Loco Hirers 20/36 locos had been reconditioned and sold as 25/36 H.P. in the previous year.

The frame of these diesel types is the same as the petrol engined 20/35 H.P. type.

Number Series (built between 1930 and 1945)

      20 H.P.: 5601-5622.

      20/36 H.P.: 5623-5648.
      Note: 5634-5638, 5640 & 5641 were PLH locos, which were reconditioned and sold as 25/36 H.P.

      25/36 H.P.: 5649-5662, 5663-5697, 5711-5725, 6501-6521.
      Note: 6501-6521 were fitted with Dorman 2DL engines. Frame type unknown.

A 4-ton 20/36 H.P. loco. The exhaust whistle can just be seen protruding from under the side of the engine cover. The cab is an optional fitting available on all Motor Rail surface locos. The one shown here is an early style and of wooden construction with a double-skinned roof for use in hot climates.

65/85 H.P.

This 10-Ton loco, w/n 5511 was shown in the 1932 catalogue as 65/85 H.P. but was listed in the order books as 60 H.P. It was quite an advanced design when compared with the company's other locos of the period and was the only one of its type built. It suffered from problems with the transmission and apparently spent most of its time upside down on the shop floor. Despite being featured in the company's 1932 catalogue and used in an advertisement on the cover of the "Locomotive, Railway Carriage & Wagon Review" of September 1932, the loco never sold and was scrapped at the works.

It had (for Motor Rail) a unique wheel arrangement with six wheels. The transmission was a 4-speed constant mesh gearbox, connected to a worm and wheel gearbox on the centre axle by a cardan shaft. The drive was transmitted from the centre axle to the front and rear axles by roller chains. It was a diesel type, equipped with Dorman's 4RBL engine that was started by a petrol donkey engine. At least one customer (Colonial Sugar refining Co. Ltd.) was also offered this locomotive in petrol and paraffin powered form using a 4-cylinder petrol engine of 6762-cc capacity.

Braking was by means of the usual screw operated type, working on the four outer wheels and a foot operated transmission brake.

Number Series (built c1930)
    5511.

Works photograph of the 65/85 H.P. loco.

44

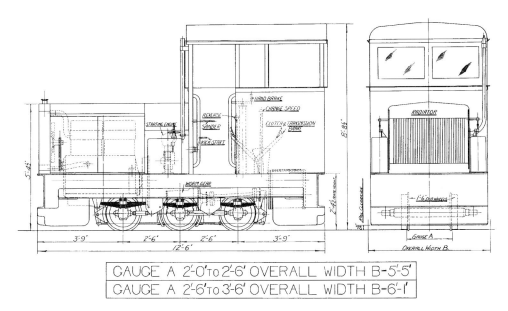

Drawing of the 65/85 H.P. loco. Scale 1:48

Fowler Engined Locos

Only two locos were built with engines from this manufacturer. Both were diesels.

5551 was fitted with a 12/18 H.P. F2V engine No. CI 158, classed as 24 H.P. and was despatched on 3rd August 1932 for Imperial Chemical Industries at Tunstead, Derbyshire as their loco number R.S. 34. The engine was later replaced by a Dorman 2DL. An entry on the engine record sheet for this loco under "special observations" states: " Mr. T. D. Abbott tested engine whilst self was away on holiday."

5552 was a metre gauge loco, classed as 20 H.P., fitted with a Fowler-Sanders M6D2-2B engine and was ordered by John Fowler (Leeds) Ltd. for an overseas location via Messrs R. Steinmann & Co. and despatched to British Guyana on 19th May 1937 via the S.S. Arakana, West Harrington Dock, Liverpool.

Number Series (built between 1932 and 1937)

    5551 - 5552.

Many people believe that the "Simplex" loco is capable of going on forever. Certainly in the right hands it needed little attention and the minimum of spare parts. There is the story which was circulating some years back of the loco owner who, when finding he had need of spares for the fourth time in twenty years was reported to have said "Motor Rail will be sick to death of us keeping popping up to Bedford every five years for a new set of brake blocks!"

Unpublished article for "On the Track," Motor Rail's in-house magazine.

12/16 H.P.

The 12/16 H.P. type was introduced in 1932, being available as either a 2½-ton or 3½-ton version. It was fitted with the Ailsa Craig DD2 2-cylinder diesel engine of 3⅞-in bore and 5½-in stroke. The DD2 was Ailsa Craig's first true diesel engine (as opposed to lamp started semi-diesels) and produced 13¼ B.H.P. at 1000 R.P.M. and 16 B.H.P. at 1500 R.P.M.

The first of these locos was supplied to the Birmingham, Tame & Rea District Drainage Board and was despatched from Bedford on 24th March 1932. As can be seen from the drawing below, the frame is the same type as used on the 20/35 H.P. petrol locos.

Number Series (built between 1932 and 1935)

    5801-5813, 5819.
    Note: 5819 was a renumbering of 5814 and 5812 was a renumbering of 5810.

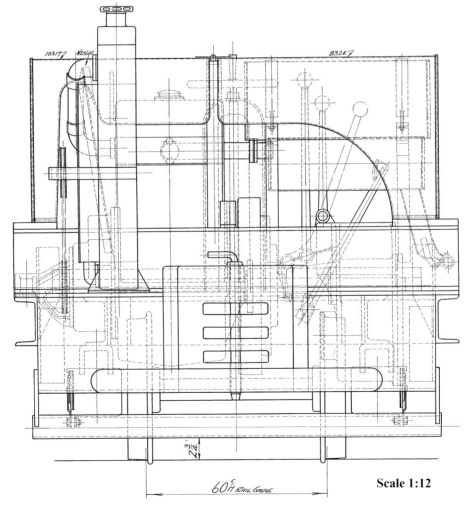

Front elevation of a 2½-Ton 12/16 H.P. loco. The radiator is offset to suit the engine fan drive pulley.

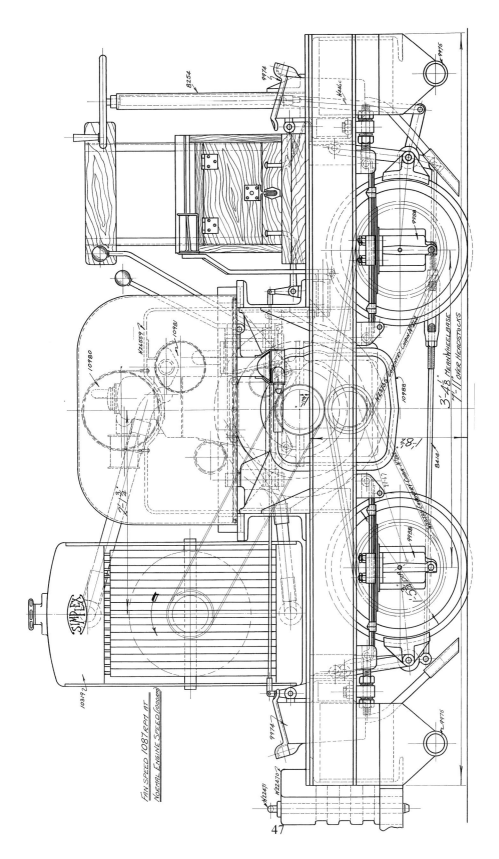

Side elevation of a 2½-Ton 12/16 H.P. loco. Scale 1:12

47

32/42 H.P.

The class 32/42 H.P. actually comprised two types that were built at different times with different engines but similar outward appearance – both are grouped together here under the same heading.

2RBL Engine

The first 32/42 H.P. types were introduced in 1932 and were illustrated in the 1932 catalogue with only a 5-Ton model being available. The first of these machines, starting at w/n 5901 was despatched on 22nd June 1932 to Joseph Boam Ltd., Middleton Towers, Norfolk for use in their sand quarries. These early locos were powered by the Dorman 2RBL diesel engine.

Number Series (built between 1932 and 1938)

    5-Ton - 5901-5915, 5197-5920, 6-Ton - 5931-5933, 5-Ton - 5941-5948, 5950-5951, 7-Ton - 5949.

A 5-Ton 32/42 H.P. loco of the early type fitted with the 2RBL engine and two speed gearbox.

2DL Engine

By 1938, a new type of 32/42 H.P. loco had been introduced. This had the Dorman 2DL engine and was offered in variants ranging from 3 to 7 Tons. The new locos generally had deeper frame channels and 3-speed gearboxes with a gated gear change lever as the most obvious visual differences from the old type.

Above is w/n 7801, supplied to ICI for Cowdale Quarry, Hindlow. It is the 7-Ton version of the later type of 32/42 H.P., illustrating the cast weights fitted to the frame tops. Note the deeper frame channel as compared to the 2RBL engined loco in the previous photo.

The 6-Ton and 7-Ton models derived some of their extra weight from large castings bolted on top of the frame ends, which acted as a shield for the driver or shunter and formed the lower half of the drivers cab where one was fitted.

When a 32/42 H.P. loco was required for gauges over 2-ft 5⅜-in the frame was very different and used a shallower section channel.

Note: Frame channel sizes are known to vary between 32/42 H.P. locos and this may have been due to such factors as availability of steel, rail gauge, etc.

<u>Number Series</u> (built between 1938 and 1958)

6522-6540, 7701-7711, 7801-7818, 7901-7999, 10001-10095, 10097-10336, 10340-10366, 10370-10457, 10464-10476.

Note: Although works number 10678 does not appear in any known company records, this loco was noted by Frank Jux under construction at the works of G. W. Bungey at Heston Aerodrome in 1954. It is possible that Bungey did erect this loco for Motor Rail or that it was a rebuild of an earlier, unidentifiable loco.

A late 32/42 H.P. loco of the 10xxx series, incorporating a new design of ballast weights. This loco is fitted with electric lighting and an overall canopy for use in tropical climates.

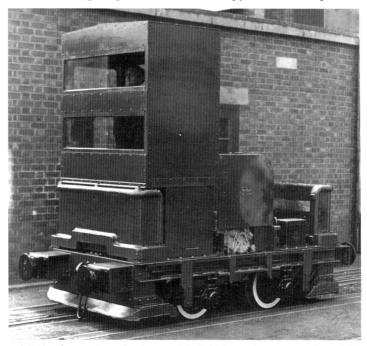

A 32/42 H.P. loco with the frame type for locos of 2-ft 8⅜-in and over stands outside the boiler house. This loco has an experimental tall cab to allow the driver to operate the controls either seated or standing without leaning out.

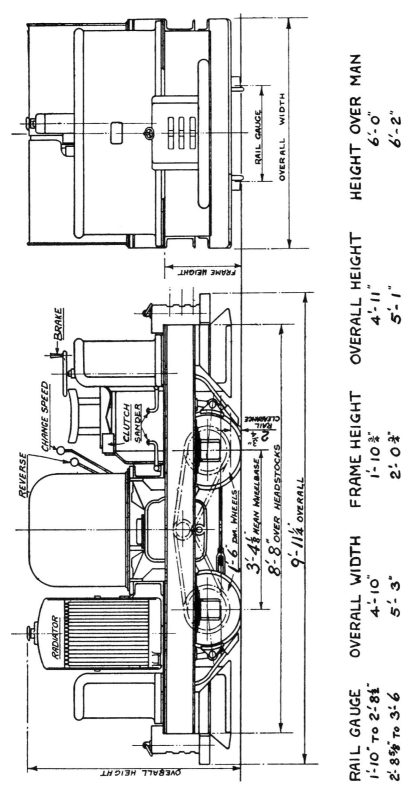

Drawing of an RB engined 7-Ton 32/42 H.P. loco. Scale 1:24

RAIL GAUGE	OVERALL WIDTH	FRAME HEIGHT
1'-10" TO 2'-8¼"	4'-10"	1'-10¾"
2'-8⅝" TO 3'-6	5'-3"	2'-0¾"

OVERALL HEIGHT	HEIGHT OVER MAN
4'-11"	6'-0"
5'-1"	6'-2"

20/28 H.P.

The 20/28 H.P. model was another of the so-called "plate frame" types. However, not all 20/28s were plate framed, those over 2-ft 6½-in gauge were built with straight channel frames. The 20/28 was the most common type produced and was built between 1933 and 1960, initially being available as 2½ and 3½-ton variants. A 4½-ton model was added later.

The 20/28 was fitted with a Dorman diesel engine, initially the 2HW, then the 2DW and finally the 2DWD. Initially Motor Rail had an exclusive licence to use these engines in their locomotives. The 2HW was built under the Ricardo licence of Messrs. Ricardo & Co. Engineers (1927), having a flat top piston and indirect fuel injection. This engine was fitted with heater plugs for cold starting, whereas the later types could be started from cold without heaters.

Other optional fittings were available as already mentioned, such as the cab etc. but the 20/28, being a diesel, could also be fitted with an exhaust conditioner for use underground. A cooling water circulating pump was an optional fitting for operation in hot climates.

The above illustration is from a spare parts list circa 1938 and clearly shows the additional ballast weights under the frame ends indicating that this is a 3½-ton loco.

The basic design remained unaltered until the mid 1950s, when a few changes were made. The most obvious of these were a new type of axlebox, heavier chains and axles, and the fully welded construction of the frame, this having previously been partially riveted.

Also in the mid 1950s, a new variation of 20/28 H.P. loco was introduced mainly for mining use in overseas markets; this was the short-framed version which introduced several features that were to be used on the 30 H.P. (later 40S) loco including the frame, new style radiator and a lever-operated brake. The short frame was primarily introduced to ensure the loco could be lowered down mineshafts with small cages, and it also allowed a greater number of locomotives to be packed into shipping containers. The old style of engine covers was retained initially but was later replaced with the style that would be used on the 40S. Some of the early short-framed 20/28s had the brakes operated by a vertically mounted wheel that was linked by means of a chain.

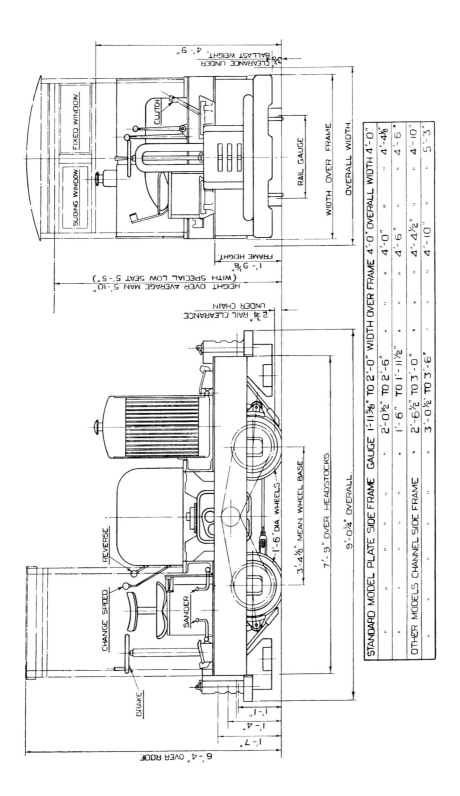

The Drawing above is taken from a sales leaflet of 1950 and shows the curved cab roof and the different heights available. Scale 1:28

STANDARD MODEL PLATE SIDE FRAME	GAUGE 1'-11⅜" TO 2'-0"	WIDTH OVER FRAME 4'-0"	OVERALL WIDTH 4'-0"
	2'-0½" TO 2'-6"	4'-0"	4'-4⅛"
	1'-6" TO 1'-11½"	4'-6"	4'-6"
OTHER MODELS CHANNEL SIDE FRAME	2'-6½" TO 3'-0"	4'-4½"	4'-10"
	3'-0½" TO 3'-6"	4'-10"	5'-3"

The standard 2¼-ton partially riveted frame 20/28 H.P. loco.

W/n 9792 is an example of a channel framed 20/28 H.P. loco. (David Hall)

A welded frame 20/28 with upgraded running gear and exhaust conditioner for mining use in South Africa.

A short-framed 20/28 with built in ballast, vertical brake wheel, new style radiator and low driver's seat. This example was supplied to South Africa via E. C. Lenning (Pty.) Ltd.

A short-framed 20/28 with bolt-on ballast weights and lever brake. This loco also has various optional extras such as electric lighting, cooling water pump for hot climates, and short cab.

In addition to the usual Dixon-Abbott type gearbox, some of the late short-framed locos were fitted with "Simtran" transmission from 1960. This system incorporated a Vulcan-Sinclair fluid coupling and a constant mesh gearbox within which the clutches were worked by hydraulics so that the action of the clutch and change speed lever was operated by one lever only. There were two versions, the single speed and the twin speed. The Simtran locos were also provided with automatic chain lubrication, which was operated by the change-direction lever.

A Simtran-equipped loco. Note the single gear operating lever for forward/reverse selection and the foot-operated engine speed control. By the time this loco had been introduced, the 20/28 H.P. had evolved into the 40S in all respects except the engine type.

A 4½-Ton Simtran loco with side panel lifted (by strategically placed screwdriver) to show the gearbox arrangement. The Simtran gearbox is a tight squeeze in a 20/28 and this necessitated the placing of the exhaust higher up, thus the hole cut in the hinged body panel. The 2DWD engine has also to be raised by approximately 2-in, this being done using packing pieces underneath the engine bearers, one of which is clearly visible in the previous photograph.

Number Series (built between 1933 and 1960)

5851-5889, 7101-7228, 7301-7499, 8501-8991, 9200-9359, 9362-9367, 9369-9378, 9380-9386, 9390, 9392-9395, 9397-9396, 9404, 9409-9422, 9424-9426, 9430-9431, 9433-9439, 9442, 9449-9450, 9455-9525, 9527-9548, 9551-9638, 9641-9667, 9669-9671, 9673-9678, 9681-9780, 9784-9788, 9790-9838, 9840-9851, 9853-9857, 9859-9861, 9863-9902, 9951-10000, 20001-20036, 20052-20061, 20062-20089, 20500-20510, 20531-20591, 21000-21292, 21295, 21500-21553, 21555-21575, 21578-21604, 21606-21636, 24011-24013, 24023-24026.

Note 1: 24xxx locos were fitted with Simtran transmission, the first of which was supplied in 1960.
Note 2: 9200-9250 were locos from the 8501-8991 series, repurchased as war surplus and given new works numbers.
Note 3: 9539, 9540, 9660-9667 were second hand locos (some were 20/26 H.P. type originally), reconditioned, fitted with new engines and given new works numbers.
Note 4: Although works numbers 20511-20530 do not appear in any known company records, three locos (20511, 20515 & 20516) were noted by Pete Roberts under construction at the works of G. W. Bungey at Heston Aerodrome in 1954. 20511, 20512 and 20513 were similarly noted by Fred Pugh in the same year. It is possible that Bungey did erect these locos for Motor Rail or that they were rebuilds of unidentifiable locos which were given new numbers in the Motor Rail series.

16/24 H.P.

The 16/24 H.P. type comprised two batches of locos that were very different in appearance but were equipped with similar engine types. This was the twin-cylinder Ailsa Craig DF2, CFS2 and later RFS2 diesel of 4½-in bore and 5½-in stroke. So as far as Motor Rail were concerned they were the same class. Motor Rail were the first customers to receive Ailsa Craig's new monobloc engines, such as the CF, as opposed to the earlier DF engine with separate crankcase and block.

Number Series

> 5821-5832 (built between 1934 and 1938).
>
> Note: This batch was of the channel-framed variety, using the same frame as the 20/35 H.P. type. Only one survives in the UK today, this being 5821 at the Bala Lake Railway in Wales.
>
> 7601-7614 (built between 1939 and 1940).
>
> Note: These were of the plate-framed variety (like the 20/28 H.P.), and were thought to have been fitted with RFS2 engines. They were visually different to the 20/28 in that they were right hand drive. None survive in the UK.

An Ailsa Craig powered loco, probably a 16/24 H.P. (Courtesy of Chris Kisch)

8/12 H.P.

The first 8/12 appeared in 1936. At only 2-Tons, this was one of the smallest Motor Rail designs. The design had a number of unusual features, although it adhered to the usual Simplex layout. It was one of only two Simplex designs to be fitted with a single cylinder engine, this being the Ailsa Craig CF1 diesel with Acro-type combustion chamber. This is the single cylinder version of the engine fitted to 16/24 H.P. locos. The engine was cooled by a water tank rather than a radiator, this being carried at the front of the loco giving it a very distinctive appearance, immediately distinguishable from other types. Another unusual feature not seen on other types was the running gear arrangement, which had the axleboxes running in adjustable horn guides, the boxes themselves supporting the frames on volute type suspension springs rather than the leaf springs usually found on Motor Rails. Most other features were similar to larger locos, including a two speed reversing gearbox, single dry plate clutch and braking applied by handwheel to all four wheels. Only twenty-three of the type were built, eight of these for the River Great Ouse Catchment board. Only three were exported.

Number Series (built between 1936 and 1949)

7501-7523.

Note:7506-7510 fitted with exhaust conditioners for contractor's use.

Length over headstocks: 7' 3"
Width over frames: 3' 9"
Mean wheelbase: 3' 1¼"
Overall height: 4' 5"
Wheel diameter: 1' 6"

8/12 H.P. Single Cylinder Diesel Loco. Scale 1:32

In the early 1960s, we had one of the Motor Rail Simplex locomotives from the Eclipse Peat Company in the West Country back for a new engine to be fitted. The (then) latest RL engine, based on the CF crankcase, went straight in, no problem. We tested it up and down the concrete drive. It rutted the drive!

Robert Kisch, Ailsa Craig Ltd.

An 8/12 (probably w/n 7518) fitted with tropical wooden cab, at Simplex Works.

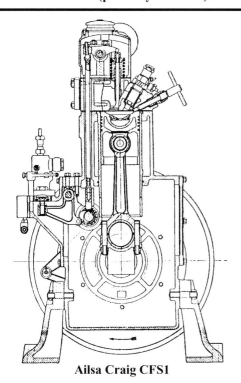

Ailsa Craig CFS1

The
Ailsa Craig
Diesel

Founded in 1891, Ailsa Craig of Chiswick, London (later Ashford, Kent) had a high reputation for economy and reliability in marine engines, but in the 1930s they were diversifying into the industrial market for small diesels.

What users say: "The engine is running beautifully silent, so that the boat is not heard at 20 Metres distance. Vibrationless, not one stay or rope moves on the 72-ft mast when the engine is in motion," Mr. P. J. Mardesic, Split, Yugo-Slavia.

48/63 H.P.

These locos are sometimes referred to as 9-Ton types and there were many variations on the theme but all used the same distinctive welded frame made from 1¼-in steel plate.

Only one of this type, w/n 9010 was used in Britain, the rest being exported. The engine used was the Dorman 3DL diesel engine and some individual locomotives were also recorded as 63, 65, 48/70 or 65/85 H.P. Transmission was by a 3-speed gearbox giving speeds of 3.2, 5.39 and 8.6 M.P.H. in the majority, with a few using a two-speed Simtran gearbox.

Standard 48/63 H.P. type (w/n 14036) for surface operation. Note the driving position, in which the driver's feet sit inside the frame. Various types of engine covers were produced, including full-length covers on some locos. Early locos had a step cut out of the frame at one end only.

Two frame widths were used depending on the rail gauge. Locos of 2-ft to 2-ft 11-in gauge had 5-ft wide frames. Locos of 2-ft 11½-in to 3-ft 6-in had a frame 6-ft wide and also had lower profile engine covers and radiator (see drawing). In the wider framed locos the conventional Simplex in-line engine and gearbox arrangement was used but this was not possible on the narrower locos. Therefore for the smaller gauges the drive from the engine was taken over the top of the gearbox to a special drop-box fitted to the outside of the gearbox. This resulted in a lower-mounted gearbox and a higher-mounted engine. A mining version was produced and was fitted with an exhaust conditioner for this purpose. The driving position on the mining version had the driver sitting further inside the frames and this, along with the exhaust conditioner and Westinghouse air brakes, made this version appear very different.

A small number of locos built to this frame type (14061 onwards) were fitted with the Dorman 4LB engine and were recorded as 85 H.P. with the final two being recorded as 85S.

9007-9018, 9022-9035, 9040-9071, 9073-9085, 9091-9100, 14001-14019, 14023-14062, 85/9/S063, 85/9/S064.

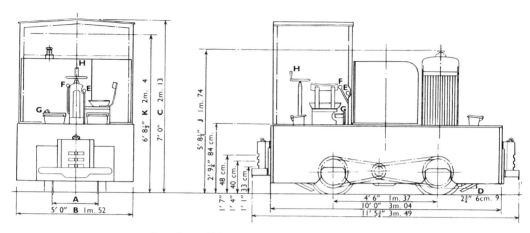

Standard 48/63 H.P. locomotive. Scale 1:48

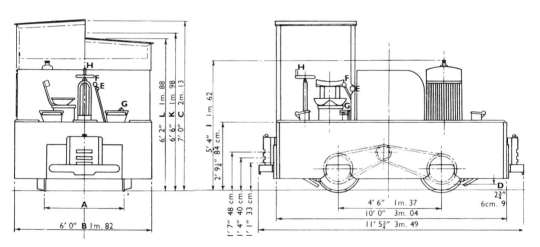

9-Ton loco for gauges 2-ft 11½-in to 3-ft 6-in. Scale 1:48

George Bungey was an old friend – he set himself up at Heston Airport after the war to recondition anything he could get his hands on including war surplus Simplexes. He used to come down regularly with an enormous list of spares for reconditioning things. I used to put in the records "this loco was Bungeyed in 195x". That was my expression for b****r it up, because he wasn't fussy about what he did.

On most locomotives there was a case where you could move the wheels in or out to various gauges but there was a gap where you couldn't get that gauge. A customer stated he had a loco of a rogue gauge, but it turned out it had been Bungeyed by moving the wheels over on one side only.

Peter Cross

View showing the installation of the 3DL engine and radiator. Notice that the driver sits on the opposite side of the loco to the engine, a characteristic unique to the 9-Ton and 10-Ton Simplex locos.

Mining version of the 9-Ton loco for South Africa via E. C. Lenning.

60S

The 60S was intended as the replacement to the 32/42 H.P. type and was originally known as the 50 H.P. before the introduction of the new numbering scheme. The frame was of all-welded construction and the minimum weight available was 4-Tons although extra ballast weights could be bolted to the frame ends to give weights up to 7-Tons. The 60S retained the traditional transverse engine and Dixon-Abbott gearbox arrangement of previous locos but the box was a three-speed version which gave speeds from 2 to 12 M.P.H. This enabled loads of up to 152-Tons to be hauled on the level (rolling resistance 15 lbs/Ton) in first gear according to a 1950s MR brochure. The type was initially fitted with the Dorman 3LA engine which was later replaced by the 3LB of 60 B.H.P. and then the 3LD of 72 B.H.P., all of these engines being water-cooled. Later water-cooled locos can be recognised by their smaller cab windows, which have curved aluminium frames as on the subsequent air-cooled locos.

In the mid 1970s, the 60S faced the problem of its engine no longer being produced and the company turned to Deutz for a new standard power unit – this was supplied in the form of the F4L912 and F4L912(W). Locomotives with the new engine were designated 60SD. The bodywork was also redesigned along the lines of the new style applied to the 40S at this time. A water-cooled engine, the Perkins 4.236, was available as an option. Only one loco was ever built with this option, this being the last Simplex built at Bedford, w/n 40SP756 despatched on 19th August 1986 to Tanganyika Sisal Spinning.

A batch of 10 locos fitted with Lister HR4 air-cooled engines (60SL) were built in 1980 for the Bord Na Mona in Ireland for use on their 3-ft gauge peat bog systems. These locos looked very different from any other 60S with their roomy cabs, large windows and special centre couplers. The engine covers were a cut-

W/n 11001, the prototype 60S, at Amberley Museum. Note the early style cab and ballast weight for the 6-Ton version. This loco was new to Eastwoods Ltd., despatched from Simplex works on 2/3/56 at a cost of £1555.0s.0d. (David Hall)

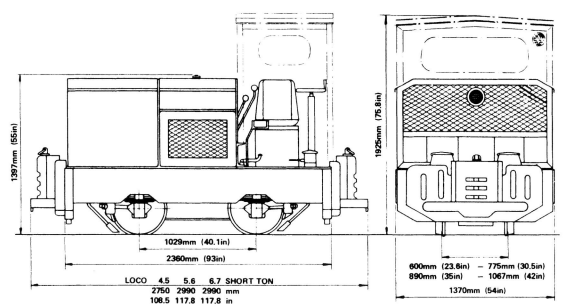

1397mm (55in)

1925mm (75.8in)

1029mm (40.1in)

2360mm (93in)

LOCO	4.5	5.6	6.7 SHORT TON
	2750	2990	2990 mm
	108.5	117.8	117.8 in

600mm (23.6in) — 775mm (30.5in)
890mm (35in) — 1067mm (42in)
1370mm (54in)

Drawing showing the later style of bodywork applied to the 60S. Scale 1:32

Simplex locos supplied to dealers Parry of India were fitted with special bodywork designed to make the loco's appearance more conventional. The above illustration shows a 60S with Parry bodywork. Alterations were also made to 20/28 H.P. and 32/42 H.P. locos to suit Parry's requirements.

short version of the standard air-cooled bodywork, with a footplate and handrail for carrying tools and personnel. These locos (and other wider gauge 40S and 60S models) had inside axleboxes to allow use on 3-ft gauge with the original frame width.

Two locos were built specially for use in palm oil factories, and these were known as the 40/60SD type. They combined the frame of a standard 60S, weighted to eight Tons, with the engine (F3L912) and two-speed gearbox of a 40SD.

The illustrations below show two variations on the water-cooled 60S locos.

Double roofed cab for use in hot climates. (5-Ton loco)

Full-length canopy. (7-Ton loco)

A 60SL loco, as supplied to Bord Na Mona.

Rear view of 7-Ton 60SD loco for the National Coal Board.

<u>Number Series</u> (built between 1955 and 1987)

Dorman Engined

11001-11027, 11029, 11031-11052, 11054-11314, 12001-12043, 12051-12060, 60S315-60S423, 60S624-60S643.

Note 1: 11001 was originally built as prototype loco 9904 with 32/42 style bodywork.

Note 2: Locos 11001-11004 had a slightly wider frame than the later production locos.

Deutz Engined

60SD701-719, 60SD724-738, 60SD752-755, 60SD757, 64SD722*, 64SD723*.

* These were the 40/60SD locos. A note in MR records states "They may be renumbered 40/60SD001 and 002".

Lister Engined

60SL740, 60SL743-750.

Perkins Engined

60SP756

In the past each new prototype was eagerly transported to a local gravel pit to be put through its paces and on one such occasion the rail gauge of the machine necessitated the location of a local track of 30". It was not until the loco was run down the ramp of the carrying vehicle only to fall between the rails that it was realised how easily 30" can be confused with 3'-0". A new rule was promptly made, that in future, on all internal paperwork, gauges would be expressed as 2'-6" (30"), 3'-0" (36") etc.

40S

This type was first introduced in 1958 and was first referred to in sales literature as the 30 H.P. type (and 40 H.P. as the power output was increased). It was not officially called 40S until the new numbering scheme of the mid 1960s. The S refers to the original "Simplex" design, and was necessary to distinguish the type from the new hydraulic locomotives then being introduced. For simplicity, all marques are referred to here as 40S regardless of time period.

The 40S was the successor to and was developed from the ubiquitous 20/28 H.P. type but used a new type of engine - the Dorman 2LB (initially 30 B.H.P. and later 40 B.H.P.). This was later superseded by the 2LD, developing 48 B.H.P. The frame was the same as that used on the short welded 20/28 H.P. locos and was only 75-in long (excluding buffer/couplers). The bodywork was also that used on some of the later short-framed 20/28s.

The 40S was available in weights from 2½-Tons to 5½-Tons with the additional weights being fixed on the ends of the frame. Drivers of these locomotives found one drawback to the shorter frame in that the cabs were a tight squeeze to get in to especially if the driver concerned was, should we say, well-built.

When Dorman ceased production of their smaller engines in the mid 1970's, Motor Rail had to look elsewhere for power units for their smaller locomotives. For the 40S they had already chosen the water-cooled Perkins P3.152 engine as an alternative to the Dorman in 1969, later to be called the 40SP variant. Water-cooled engines were preferred where possible due to the lucrative trade in radiator spares. The early 40SP used the same bodywork as the standard Dorman engined version but had the key difference of the radiator being mounted on the extreme edge of the frame (see photo). Unfortunately, the supply of Perkins engines

The photo above shows w/n 22045 of 1959, an early 40S with the water-cooled Dorman 2LB engine. This loco worked all its life for the London Brick Co. at their Warboys works and is now preserved as part of the Moseley Railway Trust collection. (David Hall)

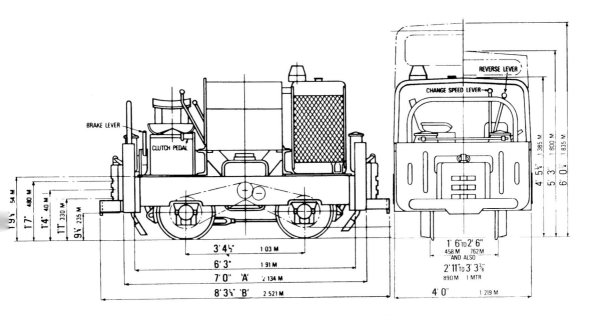

The Dorman engined 40S. Scale 1:32

proved inadequate and for the 40S the company turned to the German company Motorenfabrik Deutz A.G., whose engines had already been used in the U-Series.

With the introduction of the new Deutz F3L912 air-cooled diesel engine, the 40S range was cosmetically redesigned with full-length engine covers., The new locos incorporated SD or SP in the works number to indicate Deutz and Perkins engines respectively. The Deutz engine developed 44 Metric Horsepower at 2000 R.P.M. Another variant of this engine, the F3L912(W) with indirect fuel injection was fitted to locos for underground use. This variant developed 37 Metric Horsepower at 2000 R.P.M.

Some 40SD locos were built with only half length engine covers after a request from Severn-Trent Water Authority, whose workshops had modified the first 40SD themselves so that a second man could be carried to stop traffic at level crossings on Severn-Trent's Minworth Water Treatment Works system. This loco was used in several SMH publicity shots but was always shown from the cab end as the unofficial modification had been carried out before SMH had a chance to photograph it.

There was one more bodywork style fitted to the 40S, that of a one-off steam outline. Works number 22224 was given an American "Wild West" look, complete with "boiler" and cow-catcher for use on a pleasure railway in Wicksteed Park, Kettering. Its overall appearance was loosely based on a Union Pacific 4-4-0 loco. The frame was extended at the front, with a ballast weight at the rear and the engine covers took on the appearance of a firebox.

Shortly after the announcement that Ruston and Hornsby were ceasing manufacture of narrow-gauge loco-motives in early 1968, a copy of Motor Rail's staff magazine "On the Track" announced that the company was planning to build 40S locos fitted with the Ruston 3YWA engine, but the first customer, United Planta-tions Palm Oil Estates of Malaysia, subsequently cancelled the order and records do not indicate that any locos were actually built with this engine.

<u>Number Series</u> (built between 1958 and 1987)

Dorman Engined
22001-22260, 25011-25017, 40S261-309, 40S313-369, 40S372-449

Deutz Engined
40SD501-507, 40SD515-517, 40SD524-530.

Perkins Engined
24511, 40S310, 40S311, 40S370, 40S371, 40SP500, 40SP508-514, 40SP518-521, 40SPF522, 40SP523.

Note 1: Motor Rail records show a 4½-Ton loco number 24511 with a Perkins engine and Simtran transmission built around 1960. This loco, if it was actually built would have probably used the short welded frame and so is included here in the 40S section.
Note 2: 40SPF522 of 1981 was a flameproofed loco.
Note 3: 25xxx locomotives were fitted with Simtran transmission, the first of which was delivered in 1961.

Motor Rail's only steam-outline loco was "CHEYENNE," a modified 40S supplied in 1966 to Wicksteed Park in Kettering, where it remains to this day.

The photo above shows w/n 40SD529 of 1984, the last loco to be built at Bedford for a U.K. customer. Note the redesigned engine covers and the new more comfortable driver's seat. The loco was supplied new to Severn Trent Water Authority's Stoke Bardolph Sewage Works. (David Hall)

Perkins engined 40S – note extreme offset radiator (probably 40S310).

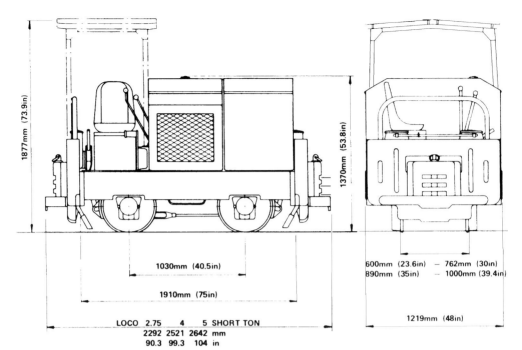

LOCO 2.75 4 5 SHORT TON
2292 2521 2642 mm
90.3 99.3 104 in

600mm (23.6in) — 762mm (30in)
890mm (35in) — 1000mm (39.4in)

1030mm (40.5in)

1910mm (75in)

1219mm (48in)

Deutz engined 40SD. Scale 1:32

40S302, a 3½-Ton 40S with inside axleboxes as used on gauges greater than 2-ft 6-in. This loco was delivered new in 1967 to Fisons at Hatfield for their 3-ft gauge peatworks system.

100 H.P.

This model was a more powerful, heavier (10-Ton) and more modern looking version of the 48/63 H.P. loco and used what was basically the same frame. It was fitted with a 5-cylinder Dorman 5LB engine, which produced 65 H.P. at 1000 R.P.M. and 113 H.P. at 1800 R.P.M. The same 3-speed transmission was used as in the 48/63 H.P. type. At least one example, 23013, was fitted with short engine covers.

Number Series (built between 1958 and 1959)
        23011-23014.

10-Ton 100 H.P. locos in the yard at Bedford. The lower one appears to have acquired an extra gear lever in its sander!

10 H.P.

This was the smallest type of loco ever produced by Motor Rail and was, according to the May 1963 edition of The Contract Journal, "specially developed for use in tunnels and mine galleries and for applications where axle loading must be kept to a minimum." At Bedford, it was affectionately known as the "Mini Simplex" or "Duplex."

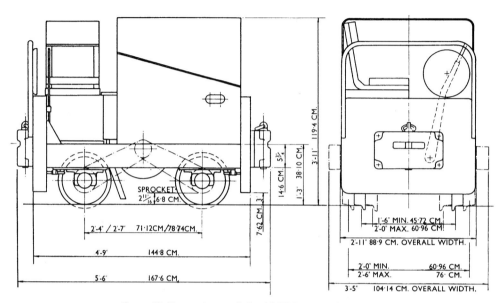

Overall dimensions of the 10 H.P. loco. Scale 1:24

The power unit of these locos was the Lister SL2 (and later SR2) air-cooled diesel engine, which produced $10\frac{1}{2}$ H.P. at 2000 R.P.M. and this was coupled to an epicyclic gearbox by means of vee belts. This gearbox gave one speed in either direction with the forward/reverse and neutral being operated by hydraulically activated cone clutches. The brake was cable operated to an expanding drum fitted on the final drive shaft of the gearbox. The wheels and axleboxes were supplied by Allens of Tipton, a firm better known for making wagons.

Haulage capacity of these locos, that only weighed in at $1\frac{3}{4}$-Tons, was given as 27-Tons on the level, going down to just 2.3-Tons on a gradient of 1 in 15.

Optional extras that could be supplied were: electric start, electric lighting (with or without battery), cab or canopy, exhaust conditioner (naked flame mines only). The type designation was later changed to 12 H.P. and with the introduction of the SR engine it was renamed 15 H.P.

Number Series (built between 1963 and 1968)

26001-26007 (10 H.P.), 26008-26016 (12 H.P.), 26017-26022 (15 H.P.).

A 10 H.P. on test at a Leighton Buzzard sand quarry.

In about 1975 we had a problem on the U-Series hydrostatics for Canada, where a batch of motors all started blowing their end caps off. Rustons said it was nothing to do with them and it must be to do with the pressure limits being exceeded by momentary peak pressures under braking. We couldn't measure these peaks with our equipment so The Cranfield Institute of Technology got involved. We instrumented and tested a loco at Bedford, but we couldn't get anything like the peak pressures quoted. So we took the loco to Leighton Buzzard and coupled it up to a train of loaded skips on a downhill gradient. In order to generate the pressure, it was necessary to get the train going and then use the hydraulic brake suddenly to stop the loco wheels. The loco was wired up with about 49 transducers and a solid cable to the Cranfield instrument box.

It was a cold and wet day and before we were really ready, someone volunteered to give it a try. He set off down the gradient and slammed the brakes on. A couple of us ran alongside feeding out the cable. Although the brakes worked perfectly as predicted, with the weight of the train, the wet rails and the gradient the wheels locked solid, the loco started to skid and the whole train carried on down the hill. We kept feeding out the wire until there was none left to feed out. Then the inevitable happened, the cable snapped. We had to solder 49 pieces of wire back together on site. In the end it turned out to be nothing to do with these pressure peaks. Our inspector went over to Rustons and discovered that the bearings in the motors weren't being shimmed-up properly.

John Palmer

40H

Although the Simtran-powered S-Series locos had been made available earlier, the 40H was Motor Rail's first attempt at a locomotive with fully hydraulic transmission and was produced at a time when the company was under considerable pressure from its South African distributors for a narrow hydraulic model for use in mines. This hydrostatic design comprised a hydraulic pump connected to the engine and a hydraulic motor connected by roller chains to the wheels. The loco emerged from the works in 1966, although only one was ever built.

It was fitted with 40 H.P. Dorman 4DA diesel No. AF 82564 and was built to 600-mm gauge (converted to 750-mm gauge before sale), weighing in at 3-Tons 19-cwt. It was sold in February 1967 for a tunnelling contract in Sweden via Carl Strom A.B. (MR agents of Stockholm, Sweden). The loco was employed by Nya Asfalt AB (New Asphalt Ltd.) in the construction of Stensjfallets Power Station, 120 km North West of Stersund. Nya Asfalt joined up with Svenka Vg A.B. (Swedish Road Ltd.) in 1982 to form Johnson Construction Company (J.C.C.) The loco was placed in storage at a J.C.C. storage site in Stockholm and is believed to have been scrapped.

Number Series (built 1966)

    40H001.

40H001 re-gauged and ready for despatch, 14th February 1967.

U-Series

The U-Series was a great change in design for Motor Rail, brought about by the South African take-over; it was the first production type to use hydraulic transmission. Originally known as the Type 10, the first U-Series locos were built for INCO (International Nickel Co.) of Canada in 1966, with an order of three going initially and being followed by a further order for thirty units a year later.

These first locos were fitted with hydrokinetic transmission (using a Brockhouse torque converter) and Dorman 4DA engines. As will be seen from the table, a great variety of engines and transmission options were used over the years. The U-Series was simple to drive, with just one lever controlling the direction, engine speed, and air brakes. Air brakes were an optional fitting and a screw-operated hand brake was the usual system. The U was produced in weights from 5 Long Tons to 10 Long Tons.

A look at the driver's controls can identify the type of transmission fitted to a loco. The hydrokinetics have what looks like a gated gear lever and the hydrostatics have a simple swinging lever. Also, the hydrostatic motor can be seen between the frames on one side of the loco.

U-Series locos had various innovations used on them such as radio control, which was fitted to the 123U type. The radio control used a portable pack that was fitted to the driver's waist and was suitable for underground use due to a guide wire that was slung from the roof of the roadway and formed an inductive loop between the locomotive and the operator's aerials. This system meant that there was no loss of signal around

Type	Engine	Transmission
110U	Dorman 4DA	Hydrokinetic
111U	Dorman 4DA	Hydrokinetic
112U	Dorman 4DA	Hydrokinetic
114U	Ruston 3YDA	Hydrokinetic
115U	Dorman 4DA	Hydrostatic
116U	Dorman 4DA	Hydrostatic
117U	Deutz F4L912	Hydrokinetic
118U	Deutz F6L912	Hydrokinetic
119U	Dorman 4DA	Hydrostatic
120U	Deutz F4L812	Hydrostatic
121U	Deutz F4L812	Hydrostatic
122U	Dorman 6DA	Hydrokinetic
123U	Deutz F4L812	Hydrostatic
124U	Dorman 4DA	Hydrokinetic
126U	Deutz F4L912	Hydrostatic

The F4L812 engined machines were for underground use. Other Deutz engined machines were for surface use.

Types 110U-114U had Brockhouse torque converters; other Hydrokinetics had Twin Disc manufacture 400 series torque converters.

All hydrostatic transmissions had Dowty "Dowmatic" variable displacement hydraulic pumps and Ruston motors.

corners. The driver always had to be within a few feet of the guide wire, and as such the system also incorporated a "dead man's" facility. 116U038 was fitted with a different form of remote control for use in the Canadian mining industry. This system transmitted its signals directly through the rails.

Chris Bashford from the Design Office puts the remote control U-Series (123U123) through its pacess at Leighton Buzzard.

115U – note the hydrostatic transmission motor between the wheels. This is a wide gauged loco with inside axleboxes.

121U100, an 8 Short Ton hydrostatic, fitted with coupler boxes for Willison Couplers.

Some 119U locos were fitted with special reinforced side rails for use with drop-bottom "Rockflo" wagons. The rails enabled the loco to be pushed over rollers at the discharge point where the rails dropped away and the entire underside of the wagon (wheels & suspension included) dropped on a hinge to allow the contents to be discharged. These were supplied to Chambishi Mine, Zambia. Unfortunately, these locos were never used with a Rockflo installation and the side rails were removed.

Number Series (built between 1966 and 1982)

110U 001-003, 005-029, 032-037, 039, 040, 049, 051, 068, 080-083, 133, 134, 137-138, 150-152.
111U 057-062, 073, 115, 116.
112U 106-109, 129, 130.
114U 004.
115U 030, 031, 045, 046, 093, 094.
116U 038.
117U 041-044, 103, 104, 140, 141.
118U 052-056, 074-077, 105, 118-121, 163, 164, 170, 171, 175, 176.
119U 050, 066, 067, 078, 079, 084, 087, 088, 122, 124-127, 131, 132, 139, 153-155, 165.
120U 063-065, 069-072, 095.
121U 085, 086, 089-092, 096-102, 110-114, 117.
122U 128, 135, 136, 142, 143, 147-149, 156-159, 174.
123U 123.
124U 144-146, 160-162, 166-169, 172, 173.

Note 1: 123U123 was a temporary remote-control rebuild of 121U117, which was later regauged and sold as 121UA117

Note 2: The last four 118U locos were designated 118UW. They were fitted with Deutz F6L912W engines and exhaust quenchers for underground use.

Note 3: Some locomotives had the letter A added after the loco type identification letter in the works number. This denoted a special feature such as Rockflo side rails or remote control. For simplicity, this has been omitted from the number series listings. This note applies equally to U, T, G and H Series locos.

119U (hydrostatic) controls.

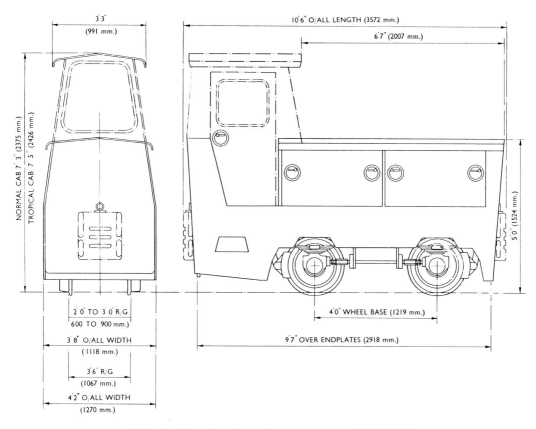

U-Series loco showing cab arrangement. Scale 1:36

117U044 (hydrokinetic) controls.

G-Series

At the time of the introduction of the G-Series in 1968, the two smallest locos in the Motor Rail range were the 15 H.P. Mini and the more traditional 40S. The G-Series was designed to meet the requirements of the State Mining Corporation of Ghana whose specification for new locomotives fell between these types. The G proved to be a success and became a standard part of the range, with the Mini locos being dropped. The first G's (100G and 101G types) were fitted with Enfield HO.85 air-cooled engines of 15 H.P. with a single plate dry clutch, coupled to a reversing gearbox by means of a belt (with the exception of 100G032 & 033, which used chains). Final drive to the axles was by roller chains. The 101G was 4-in longer than the 100G to give extra space in the cab. The 102Gs had Enfield's HO.100 (Horizontally Opposed) 2-cylinder diesel engines of 21 H.P. The 103G and 104G had redesigned frames and bodywork, with the 103G having Petter's PJ2 engine of either 15½ or 20 B.H.P. and the 104G using the Indian made 20 B.H.P. Kirloskar RA2 engine. The 105G was the only G type to use a water-cooled engine, this being the Petter PJ2-W. Weights ranged from 2 to 3 Short Tons.

The majority were exported but eight were used in the UK by British Rail (1), ICI (4), Severn-Trent Water (2) and Thyssen (G.B.) Ltd. (1).

Number Series (built between 1968 and 1984)

      100G 001-015, 032, 033.
      101G 016-025, 027.
      102G 026, 028-030.
      103G 038-055, 058, 059, 061, 062, 064-081, 086.
      104G 060, 063.
      105G 082-085.

      Note 1: 103GA078 was actually built to standard gauge for British Railways' Wolverton works.
      Note 2: 103G061 and 062 were modified and renumbered from 051 and 050 respectively.
      Note 3: 103G064 and 065 were modified and renumbered from 054 and 052 respectively. They were converted for underground use by the fitting of catalytic exhaust converters.

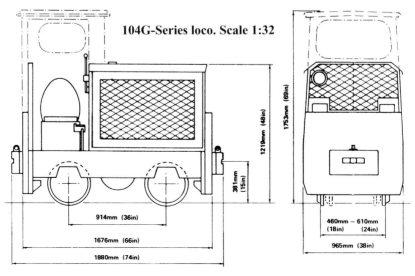

104G-Series loco. Scale 1:32

1753mm (69in)

1219mm (48in)

381mm (15in)

914mm (36in)

1676mm (66in)

1880mm (74in)

460mm – 610mm (18in) (24in)

965mm (38in)

One of the 104G locos (104G063) of Severn-Trent Water, Newstead Works, Stoke-on-Trent.

101G Enfield-engined loco in the yard at Bedford. Note the newly-introduced Motor Rail logo fitted to the air intake at the front.

H-Series

The H-Series was intended to be an eventual replacement for the 40S in the same way that the U had been intended to replace the 60S, but the H proved too expensive and in the end only five were built. The H-Series looked similar in style to the U-series but it was much shorter and had the feature of a fold-up driving well so that the loco could be lowered down a mineshaft with ease.

The first H-Series was ordered on 23rd February 1968 and was intended for British Newfoundland Exploration Ltd., Badger, Newfoundland. It was to be gauged to 2-ft but the wheelsets were to be convertible to 2-ft 6-in or 3-ft gauge if necessary. This first loco was allocated w/n 100H001 but did not receive this number as the order was subsequently cancelled. It appears that this first loco, or what existed of it at the time, was used to fulfil an order from the British Aluminium Co. Ltd. for their 3-ft gauge Lochaber works line in Scotland. Changes were made, which included the fitting of a passenger seat, cab, and a hydraulic power-take-off in the form of a Dowty pump and snap-on flexible hoses. This was suitable for an Atlas digger or a ¾ cu yd end-tipping wagon. The works number given when it left the works was 105H006 although some records also refer to it as 105H001.

The four 100H type locos were sold through dealer Jarvis Clark Co. Ltd. for INCO, Thompson Mine, Canada and were also capable of being regauged from their initial 3-ft down to 2-ft, or 2-ft 6-in gauge. As they were intended for mining use, they were fitted with Oxy-France exhaust scrubbers and fail-safe air brakes. The power unit fitted to the 100Hs was the Deutz F3L812(W) of 29 B.H.P. at 1800 R.P.M., whereas the 105H had a Deutz F3L912 of 37 B.H.P. at 2300 R.P.M. All used hydrokinetic transmission in the form of

An H-Series for Canada in the works yard at Bedford. Evidence of the regaugability of this class can be seen in the design of the brake hangers.

An H-Series locomotive with the driving well folded. This shortens the locomotive considerably to fit down mineshafts.

a Brockhouse torque converter. The wheels used were the same 18-in diameter pattern as used on the 40S/60S and the drive to the axles was by chains. The price of a new H-Series locomotive in 1969 was £2431.0s.0d.

Number Series (built between 1968 and 1969)

    100H 002-005.
    105H 006.

We built a couple of U-Series locos for use with the Rockflo system for Chambishi Mine, Zambia. They had side rails built out of two inch plates specially rolled up at the edges. When they got them, they decided not to use them on the Rockflo system, but they neglected to mention this on the subsequent order and simply specified "as per previous order." It was only when I went out there a few years later that I realised that the first thing they did with every loco when they received it was to chop the side rails off.

John Palmer

T-Series

The T-Series was a diesel-hydraulic type and was similar in appearance to the U-Series but was heavier and larger in most respects including the wheel diameter (21-in on U-Series, 24-in on T-Series). Although it was designed with use as a mining loco in mind, none were actually bought for underground use. They were mostly sold for export with only two British customers, these being the National Coal Board, who used the type on the surface as stockyard shunters on 2-ft 6-in gauge systems at Allerton Bywater and Hem Heath Collieries, and Associated Portland Cement Ltd., who used one at their Kilvington Gypsum works.

During its production, the T was offered with three varieties of engine: the Dorman 6DA (air-cooled), the Deutz F6L912 (air-cooled) and the Perkins 6.354 (water-cooled). Transmission was by means of a Twin Disc 400 series torque converter coupled to a drop box, right angle gearbox and chain drive to both axles. Alternatively, a hydrostatic transmission was available, fitted with a Dowty "Dowmatic" variable displacement (swashplate) hydraulic pump, as fitted to the U-Series hydrostatics, this being connected to a Staffa motor driving by chains to the wheels.

The T-Series was available in weights from 9 to 14 Short Tons. The additional weight was achieved by varying numbers of steel slabs that were mounted on the front and rear of the frame. Many locos were fitted with air brakes in addition to a hand-wheel operated parking brake.

A 2-ft 6-in gauge 14-Ton 101T loco for N.C.B. Ledston Luck Colliery. Note the four ballast weights on the front. This loco is fitted with a remote-uncoupler that can be operated from the Driver's cab.

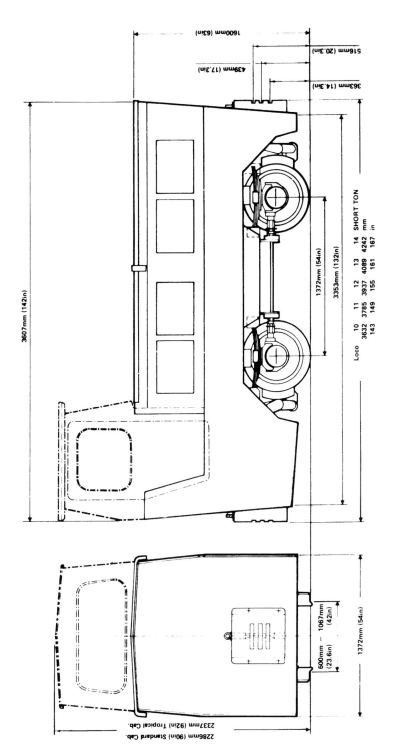

T-Series loco for 2-ft - 3-ft 6-in gauge. Scale 1:32

Loco	10	11	12	13	14	SHORT TON
	3632	3785	3937	4089	4242	mm
	143	149	155	161	167	in

Type	Weight	Engine	Transmission	Number Series (built between 1972 and 1984)
100T	12T	Dorman 6DA	Dowty Dowmatic	**100T** 001-003, 008-015.
101T	10, 14T	Dorman 6DA	Twin Disc	**101T** 018-023.
102T	12, 14T	Deutz F6L912	Twin Disc	**102T** 004-007, 016.
103T	9T	Perkins 6.354	Twin Disc	**103T** 017.

102T016 at Blue Circle Industries, Kilvington Gypsum Works, Nottinghamshire.

100Ts for Tanzania. These 12 Short Ton 600-mm gauge locos (100T008-100T015) were equipped with Dorman 6DA engines, extra large fuel tanks and auto-directional double head/tail lights.

The Alan Keef Years

Several locos derived from Simplex designs have been built in the years since the locomotive side of the business of Simplex Mechanical Handling Ltd. was sold to Alan Keef Ltd. These designs are still available today.

40S

The last locomotive to be built to an order placed with Simplex Mechanical Handling was a 40SD for Butterley Building Materials Ltd., for use at their Cherry Orchard and Star Lane Brickworks near Southend in Essex. This loco was built by Alan Keef for SMH but was given a number in the SMH series – 40SD530. It was identical in appearance to the SMH-built locos. This locomotive was built entirely at the new works at Lea Line near Ross-on-Wye.

In 1987, Alan Keef received an order for another 40S loco (Alan Keef w/n 26) from Butterley but this time the frame was extended rearward in order to fit a modern and roomy driver's cab. Alan Keef's own style of bodywork was also fitted. Other innovations were a hydraulically operated clutch and with the extra space in the cab, the old style brake wheel was reinstated in place of the lever. Another of the type was built for the same firm in 1988 (Alan Keef w/n 28) but this time the frame was lengthened in both directions to make it appear more evenly balanced.

A Keef-built 40S (AK 26) with rearward extension to frame. (David Hall)

60S

60SD757 was built to an order from Simplex Mechanical Handling and work commenced at Alan Keef's Cote site but was completed after the move to Lea Line in 1986. This loco was destined for Ghana Bauxite, was 3-ft 6-in gauge and weighed 6-Tons.

Three other locomotives have been built to the basic 60S design although the appearance of the first two of these was unlike any 60S before, having full length running boards, wide bodywork and buffer beams that were wider than the frames. Both were 3-ft 6-in gauge locos for Nigeria, w/n 29 of 1988 and w/n 36 of 1990. The third and latest 60S type to be built was w/n 43, which was exported to Guyana for use by the Guyana Sugar Corporation. All had Perkins engines.

The last Simplex built to date, Metre gauge Alan Keef w/n 43 of 1992. This 60S is unusual in being configured as a left-hand drive. (Alan Keef Ltd.)

85S

This type was based on the old 9-Ton frame types which were latterly known as 85S. Only one of these locos has been built by Alan Keef Ltd., this being w/n 37 of 1990, built for Chemicals & Fertilisers of Port Harcourt, Nigeria. It was fitted with a Perkins 6-354 engine although an Alan Keef sales leaflet of the time quoted a Ford BSD444T of 90 B.H.P.

U-Series

Two of these were built (AK 24 & 25) in 1988 for Kyung Dong Coal Mine in Korea. Both had Deutz F6L912(W) engines of 90 H.P. with hydrostatic transmission and weighed 10 Tons.

U-Series AK24 and AK25 under construction at Lea Line in March 1988. (John Rowlands)

The finished article ready for delivery to Korea, AK25 at Lea Line. (Ken Scanes)

<u>Rebuilds</u>

As well as building new locos of Motor Rail and their own designs, Alan Keef Ltd. continue to overhaul and rebuild old Motor Rail locos for various customers and have dealt with many types over the years including two T-Series locos that were purchased from British Coal and overhauled and sold for use in the building of the Channel Tunnel. One of these locos, having been bought back by Alan Keef, was rebuilt in 2000 for use as a passenger loco on the Leighton Buzzard Railway. It was given works number 59R.

The Pretenders

Many successful firms have had their products copied over the years and Motor Rail were no exception, with at least two companies copying designs or using their good name to their own advantage.

Kent Construction / F. C. Hibberd

The company most known for copying Motor Rail designs was The Kent Construction and Engineering Co. Ltd. of Ashford, Kent. This company, who used the trade name "Planet" on their locos, was sold to F. C. Hibberd and D. A. Dwyer in 1926 and subcontracted loco work successively to various firms including Baguley and Bedford Engineering until opening its own works at Park Royal, London in 1932.

Kent Construction bought up war-surplus 20 and 40 H.P. locos and rebuilt them in much the same way as MRTC and Wm. Jones. The trouble was, they sold the rebuilt locos as "Planet-Simplex" and were subject to legal proceedings by MRTC as a result. By the time that the company was known as F. C. Hibberd & Co. Ltd., they were producing complete locos that were almost identical to MRTC's 20 H.P. type but later also used diesel engines other than Dorman such as those from Davey Paxman and Co. Ltd. and The National Gas and Oil Engine Co. Ltd.

The bent-frame design continued to be produced by Hibberd until at least 1951, almost two decades after Motor Rail ceased to use the design themselves. The gearboxes for these locos were presumably bought straight from David Brown, who had made the gearboxes for the Motor Rail 20 H.P. locos, once the supply of old Motor Rail boxes had dried up. Contemporary publicity material for Planet-Simplex locos draws particular attention to a number of minor improvements made in the gearbox of the Planet locos.

A Hibberd-built 20 H.P. loco at Cumberland Moss Litter Industries. Note deep buffer beam and coupler. (A. Neale collection)

1887	1934	D. Preece, private site nr. Colne, Lancs
1896	1935	Launceston Steam Rly., Cornwall
1980	1936	Amberley Museum, W. Sussex
2163	1938	Simon Lomax, private site, Leicestershire
2306	194x	Cadeby Lt. Rly., Leicestershire
2408	1941	L&P Peat, Solway Moss, Cumbria
2586	1941	Leighton Buzzard Lt. Rly., Bedfordshire
2631	1943	Leighton Buzzard Lt. Rly., Bedfordshire
????	19??	Leighton Buzzard Lt. Rly., Bedfordshire

Surviving Hibberd bent-frame locos in Britain (MR rebuilds and new locos).

Margolis & Ralph / E. C. Lenning Pty.

E. C. Lenning (Pty.) Ltd. of Boksburg, Transvaal were agents for Motor Rail in South Africa from the 1940s and had taken over the firm of Margolis & Ralph Engineering (Pty.) Ltd. by 1959. Margolis & Ralph (M&R) had been building pirate copies of Motor Rail locos since the late 1950s and used parts from Motor Rail in

A 3½-Ton M&R loco, equipped with a Dorman 2LB engine. The transmission incorporated a Brockhouse torque converter and epicyclic forward and reverse gearbox in a single housing.

their construction.

M&R were acquired by Lenning not as would be expected to stop the pirate copies but to profit from this activity themselves. In reality, they were responding to increased local demand for locomotives in South Africa, which was extremely high at the time with gold mines being sunk in the Free State Gold Field and the discovery of the Evander Gold Field. Also, many existing mines were converting from mule to locomotive haulage at this time. So it was not surprising that mine owners wanted a locally made product when there would be delays in sourcing locos from the UK.

Initial investigations by M&R involved the replacement of the Motor Rail flywheel by a Chrysler torque converter, retaining the existing gearbox. Tom Dixon Abbott inspected one of these locos on a visit to South Africa in 1958 and concluded that this conversion was not ideal due to the low engine speed which was not a good match for the torque converter. Motor Rail abandoned the idea of torque converters, opting instead for fluid flywheels in the Simtran transmission. However, M&R persevered and eventually found the more suitable Brockhouse torque converter, which they combined with an epicyclic reversing gearbox driving down to a layshaft on which the chain sprockets were mounted. M&R also built their engine and transmission into a single unit which could be quickly removed and exchanged to keep each loco serviceable.

A busy scene inside the M&R works, with Motor Rail locos being dismantled into their component parts, many of which are then incorporated into the "new" M&R locos. The remains of a discarded Simplex gearbox can be seen in the left foreground. At the rear of the line of M&R locos can be seen an M&R 5-Ton type loco, the design of which is thought to have influenced both Motor Rail and W. G. Bagnall in their endeavours to build small hydraulic locos.

Simplexes in Industry

The following photographs show some of the varied industries and locations served in by Simplex locomotives over the years.

A Priestman navvy loads a train with sand at Joseph Arnold's Chamberlain Quarry, Leighton Buzzard on 14th August, 1968. 20/28 H.P. w/n 7403 was one of Arnold's many Simplexes. (S.Leleux)

A 2-ft 11-in gauge 32/42 H.P. loco, owned by London Brick Co. Ltd. at Newton Longville. (S.Leleux)

A slight derailment for 20/28 H.P. w/n 8810 at the gravel pits of A. J. Mackaness near Northampton. This photograph was taken in April 1962. (S. Leleux)

Ex W.D.L.R. bent frame 20 H.P. petrol loco, w/n 314. It is seen at John Browne (Bridgewater) Ltd., Chilton Trinity Tileworks, Somerset in August 1962. (S. Leleux)

20/28 H.P. w/n 7129 with overall cab and canopy. Seen here at the brickworks of Redland Flettons Ltd., Kempston Hardwick on 13th September, 1967. This loco is now preserved at the Leighton Buzzard Railway and is named "CARAVAN." (S. Leleux)

9 Ton 3-ft 6-in gauge 48/63 H.P. loco working at Ndola Copper Mines, Zambia. This loco has double Alliance couplers fitted for use both inside and outside the refinery.

20/26 H.P. w/n 4813 on the Finedon-Wellingborough sewer contract with the Conduit Construction Co. Note the empty hole in the right-hand side of the engine bearer, a sign that this loco has been fitted with a diesel engine. (S. Leleux)

A rare shot of a Simplex in use in the slate industry. 20/28 H.P., w/n 20073 is seen at work in August, 1963 on the slate waste tips at Maen Offeren near Blaenau Festiniog. (S. Leleux)

British Portland Cement, Sundon, Bedfordshire. W/n 3695 (near). This loco used the 40 H.P. petrol loco type frame but was fitted with a Fowler diesel engine from new. The buffer is a later addition from a Ruston & Hornsby loco. (S. Leleux)

Alan Keef's "DIGGER" (w/n 8882), seen here at the Rosemary Tileries, Essington works of Haunchwood-Lewis Brick & Tile Ltd. (S. Leleux)

Simplexes Today

The Simplexes remaining in industrial use in the U.K. are often very different from the day they left Elstow Road. In fact some are so different that they can only be recognised as Simplexes from their frames. These pages show some of the Simplexes that remained at work in the last decade or so of the 20th Century.

"BECKY" w/n 7215. This loco, started life as a 3½-Ton 20/28 type and was new to the Ham River Grit Co. at Bletchingley in 1938. It passed through the hands of several owners, which included spending time at Leighton Buzzard in the use of Joseph Arnold & Sons Ltd., working in their sand quarries. 7215 received a major rebuild by Alan Keef Ltd., after being left as little more than a frame and wheels at the Vale of Teifi Railway. The rebuild included all new bodywork and a new Deutz air-cooled engine. It is seen here in post-rebuild condition in 1996 in the ownership of Joseph Metcalf Ltd. on their peat works line at Chat Moss near Irlam, Manchester. (Glenn Hall)

W/n 5402. This loco is, as mentioned earlier, the oldest loco in industrial service in the U.K. at the time of writing. It started life in 1932 as a 20/35 H.P. petrol loco and was supplied to building contractors John Laing Ltd. Little is known about its further exploits until it turned up at Richardson's Moss Litter at Letham Moss, Scotland in the 1960s. By this time it had received a Dorman 2DWD engine. As can be seen it now sports a home-made cab and a Deutz engine. The photo was taken in 1998 at Letham Moss. (David Hall)

"IVOR," w/n 8678. The last loco to be used in a claypit in the U.K., it was built in 1941 as a standard 20/28 H.P. type and was originally part of the Diesel Loco Hirers Ltd. fleet. It was later sold to the Ightam Brick & Tile Co. Ltd., Kent and passed into the ownership of the Sussex & Dorking United Brick Co. Ltd. when they took over the Ightam works. At some time in the 1970s, it was sent to be rebuilt and received a cab and a 3-cylinder air-cooled Lister engine – this involved major frame surgery as can be seen in the photo. It is shown in 1997 at its current home of Wm. Blyth Ltd. at their Far Ings Tileries, Barton on Humber, Lincs. Note the lorry fuel tank. (David Hall)

And finally... your authors, Messrs. Rowlands and Hall pose with "DIGGER," 20/28 H.P. Motor Rail 8882 of 1944 at the premises of Alan Keef Ltd., near Ross-on-Wye. "DIGGER" has been works shunter and part of the Keef hire fleet for many years, being probably the most famous Simplex still in industrial service. (Patrick Keef)

Existing Simplex Locos in England, Scotland and Wales

W/n	Type	Location	Gauge	Status
264	20 H.P.	Welsh Highland Rly., Porthmadog	2-ft	
461	40 H.P.	Museum of Army Transport, Beverley	2-ft	
596?	40 H.P.	Festiniog Rly.	2-ft	
997	20 H.P.	I.B.Jolly, nr. Mold, Clwyd	2-ft	Dsm
1111	20 H.P.	Moseley Railway Trust	2-ft	
1320	40 H.P.	Cadeby Lt. Rly., Cadeby, Leics.	2-ft	
1364	40 H.P.	Imperial War Museum	2-ft	
1369	40 H.P.	Moseley Railway Trust	2-ft	
1377	40 H.P.	Leighton Buzzard Rly., Beds.	2-ft	
1381	40 H.P.	Amberley Museum, W. Sussex	2-ft	
1757	20 H.P.	Nick Williams, private rly., Reading	2-ft	
1934	20 H.P.	G. Fairhurst, nr. Bettisfield, Salop.	2-ft	
1935	20 H.P.	Skegness Water Leisure Park	2-ft	
2014	20 H.P.	Dalmunzie Hotel, Perth & Kinross	2-ft 6-in	
2059	20 H.P.	C.J & A.M.Pearman, Huntingdon	2-ft	
2097	20 H.P.	Lithgow s Ltd., Langbank, Renfrewshire	2-ft	
2171	20 H.P.	Lithgow s Ltd., Langbank, Renfrewshire	2-ft	
2197	20 H.P.	Cadeby Lt. Rly., Cadeby, Leics.	2-ft	
3663	40 H.P.	ESCA Engineering, Wigan	2-ft	
3720	20 H.P.	Amberley Museum, W. Sussex	2-ft	
3739	20 H.P.	Delabole Slate, Delabole, Cornwall	1-ft 11-in	
3797	40 H.P.	Irchester NGRT, Irchester, Northants.	3-ft	
3849	20 H.P.	Imperial War Museum, Duxford	2-ft 6-in	
3995	20 H.P.	Skegness Water Leisure Park	2-ft	
4023	20 H.P.	FMB Engineering, Hants.	2-ft	
4565	20 H.P.	Threlkeld Quarry Museum, Cumbria	2-ft	
4570	20 H.P.	Leighton Buzzard Rly., Beds.	2-ft	
4572	20 H.P.	Cadeby Lt. Rly., Cadeby, Leics.	2-ft	
4709	20/26 H.P.	J.L.Butler, Grove Heath, Surrey	2-ft	
4724	20/26 H.P.	Bursledon Brickworks, Hants.	2-ft	
4803	20/26 H.P.	I.B.Jolly, nr. Mold, Clwyd	2-ft	
4805	20/26 H.P.	Leighton Buzzard Rly., Beds.	2-ft	Dsm
5025	20 H.P.	I.B.Jolly nr. Mold, Clwyd	2-ft 7-in	Dsm
5038	20 H.P.	Cadeby Lt. Rly., Cadeby, Leics.	2-ft	Dsm
5213	20/35 H.P.	Embsay & Bolton Abbey Rly. NG Group	2-ft	
5226	20/35 H.P.	Bursledon Brickworks, Hants.	2-ft	
5260	20/35 H.P.	Abbey Pumping Stn., Leicester	2-ft	
5262	20/35 H.P.	Private site, Lancs.	2-ft	Dsm
5297	20/35 H.P.	Old Kiln Rly., Tilford, Surrey	2-ft	
5402	20/35 H.P.	L&P Peat, Letham Moss Airth, Central	2-ft	
5603	20 H.P. (D)	Leighton Buzzard Rly., Beds.	2-ft	Dsm
5608	20 H.P. (D)	Leighton Buzzard Rly., Beds.	2-ft	Dsm

W/n	Type	Location	Gauge	Status
5612	20 H.P. (D)	Leighton Buzzard Rly., Beds.	2-ft	Dsm
5613	20 H.P. (D)	Leighton Buzzard Rly., Beds.	2-ft	Dsm
5646	20/36 H.P.	Launceston Steam Rly., Cornwall	2-ft	
5713	25/36 H.P.	Old Kiln Rly., Tilford, Surrey	2-ft	
5821	12/16 H.P.	Bala Lake Rly., Gwynedd	2-ft	
5852	20/28 H.P.	I.B.Jolly, nr. Mold, Clwyd	2-ft	Dsm
5853	20/28 H.P.	Cadeby Lt. Rly., Cadeby, Leics.	2-ft	
5859	20/28 H.P.	Abbey Lt. Rly., Kirkstall, Leeds	2-ft	
5863	20/28 H.P.	Amberley Museum, W. Sussex	2-ft	
5875	20/28 H.P.	Leighton Buzzard Rly., Beds.	2-ft	Dsm
5877	20/28 H.P.	Alan Keef Ltd., Ross on Wye, Hereford	2-ft	
5879	20/28 H.P.	Alan Keef Ltd., Ross on Wye, Hereford	2-ft 6-in	
5880	20/28 H.P.	South Tynedale Rly., Alston, Cumbria	2-ft	Dsm
5881	20/28 H.P.	David White, Wibtoft , Leics.	2-ft	
5902	32/42 H.P.	East Anglian Transport Mus., Lowestoft	2-ft	Dsm
5906	32/42 H.P.	Butterley NGRA, Midland Rly. Centre	2-ft	
5912	32/42 H.P.	East Anglian Transport Mus., Lowestoft	2-ft	
6012	12/20 H.P.	Leighton Buzzard Rly., Beds.	2-ft	
6013	12/20 H.P.	I.B.Jolly, nr. Mold, Clwyd	2-ft	Dsm
6031	12/20 H.P.	Bromyard & Linton Rly., Hereford	2-ft	
6035	12/20 H.P.	Moseley Railway Trust	2-ft	
7033	20/26 H.P.	Moseley Railway Trust	2-ft	
7036	20/26 H.P.	Leighton Buzzard Rly., Beds.	2-ft	
7037	20/26 H.P.	Sinclair Horticultural, Bolton Fell, Cumbria	2-ft	
7053	20/26 H.P.	North Glos. Rly., Toddington Goods Yard	2-ft	
7057	20/26 H.P.	Romney, Hythe & Dymchurch Rly.	1-ft 3-in	
7066	20/26 H.P.	Alan Keef Ltd., Ross on Wye, Hereford	2-ft	Dsm
7105	20/28 H.P.	Leighton Buzzard Rly., Beds.	2-ft	
7108	20/28 H.P.	Leighton Buzzard Rly., Beds.	2-ft	
7126	20/28 H.P.	Vale of Teifi Rly., Llandyssul, Dyfed	2-ft	
7129	20/28 H.P.	Leighton Buzzard Rly., Beds.	2-ft	
7128	20/28 H.P.	Stevington & Turvey Rly., Beds.	2-ft	
7137	20/28 H.P.	L&P Peat, Solway Moss, Cumbria	2-ft 6-in	Dsm
7153	20/28 H.P.	Yaxham Lt. Rly., Yaxham, Norfolk	2-ft	
7188	20/28 H.P.	Sinclair Horticultural, Bolton Fell, Cumbria	2-ft	
7189	20/28 H.P.	D.Ritchie, Edinburgh	2-ft	
7190	20/28 H.P.	L&P Peat, Nutberry Moss, Dumfries	2-ft	
7191	20/28 H.P.	Threlkeld Quarry Mus., Cumbria	2-ft	Dsm
7192	20/28 H.P.	Strumpshaw Hall Steam Mus., Norfolk	2-ft	
7199	20/28 H.P.	East Hayling Lt. Rly., Hayling Island, Hants.	2-ft	
7214	20/28 H.P.	Leighton Buzzard Rly., Beds.	2-ft	
7215	20/28 H.P.	Joseph Metcalf Ltd., Chat Moss, Irlam	2-ft	
7330	20/28 H.P.	D.Ritchie, Edinburgh	2-ft	
7333	20/28 H.P.	J.Lloyd, North Yorkshire	2-ft	

W/n	Type	Location	Gauge	Status
7371	20/28 H.P.	West Lancs. Lt. Rly., Hesketh Bank, Lancs.	2-ft	
7374	20/28 H.P.	G.Feldwick, Wickford, Essex	2-ft	
7403	20/28 H.P.	S.Hodgson, Garndolbanmaen, Gwynedd	2-ft	
7463	20/28 H.P.	Levington Horticulture, Kirkbride, Cumbria	2-ft	
7469	20/28 H.P.	Great Bush Rly., Hadlow Down, E. Sussex	2-ft	
7471	20/28 H.P.	Amerton Rly., Staffs.	2-ft	
7474	20/28 H.P.	Yaxham Lt. Rly., Yaxham, Norfolk	2-ft	
7481	20/28 H.P.	Lincs. Coast Lt. Rly.	2-ft	
7493	20/28 H.P.	North Ings Farm Mus., Dorrington, Lincs.	2-ft	
7494	20/28 H.P.	Poppleton Nursery Lt. Rly., York	2-ft	
7498	20/28 H.P.	Sinclair Horticultural, Bolton Fell, Cumbria	2-ft	
7512	8/12 H.P.	Cadeby Lt. Rly., Cadeby, Leics.	2-ft	
7522	8/12 H.P.	Threlkeld Quarry Mus., Cumbria	2-ft	
7710	32/42 H.P.	Cadeby Lt. Rly., Cadeby, Leics.	2-ft	
7902	32/42 H.P.	Legoland, Windsor	2-ft	
7927	32/42 H.P.	Llanberis Lake Rly.	2-ft	Dsm
7933	32/42 H.P.	Leighton Buzzard Rly., Beds.	2-ft	
7955	32/42 H.P.	West Lancs. Lt. Rly., Hesketh Bank, Lancs.	2-ft	Dsm
7956	32/42 H.P.	Leighton Buzzard Rly., Beds.	2-ft	
8540	20/28 H.P.	J.L.Butler, Grove Heath, Surrey	2-ft	
8564	20/28 H.P.	Leadhills & Wanlockhead Rly.	2-ft	Dsm
8565	20/28 H.P.	Festiniog Rly.	2-ft	
8600	20/28 H.P.	D.Turner, "Fairhaven", Wychbold, Worcs.	2-ft	
8606	20/28 H.P.	Brett Gravel, Chartham, nr. Canterbury	2-ft	
8614	20/28 H.P.	Environmental Contractor, Dorset	2-ft	
8622	20/28 H.P.	Lincs. Coast Rly.	2-ft	
8627	20/28 H.P.	Threlkeld Quarry Mus., Cumbria	2-ft	
8640	20/28 H.P.	G.Feldwick, Wickford, Essex	2-ft	Dsm
8641	20/28 H.P.	Museum of Army Transport, Beverley	2-ft	
8644	20/28 H.P.	Abbey Lt. Rly., Kirkstall, Leeds	2-ft	S/O
8655	20/28 H.P.	Sinclair Horticultural, Bolton Fell, Cumbria	2-ft	
8663	20/28 H.P.	Moseley Railway Trust	2-ft	
8667	20/28 H.P.	Museum of Army Transport, Beverley	2-ft	
8669	20/28 H.P.	Moseley Railway Trust	2-ft	
8678	20/28 H.P.	Wm. Blyth, Far Ings Tileries, Nth. Lincs.	2-ft	
8687	20/28 H.P.	Great Bush Rly., Hadlow Down, E. Sussex	2-ft	
8694	20/28 H.P.	Bursledon Brickworks, Hants.	2-ft	
8695	20/28 H.P.	Leighton Buzzard Rly., Beds.	2-ft	
8696	20/28 H.P.	Sinclair Horticultural, Bolton Fell, Cumbria	2-ft	
8698	20/28 H.P.	Threlkeld Quarry Mus., Cumbria	2-ft	Dsm
8700	20/28 H.P.	Lithgow s Ltd., Langbank, Renfrewshire	2-ft	
8703	20/28 H.P.	Welsh Highland Rly., Porthmadog	2-ft	
8704	20/28 H.P.	Sinclair Horticultural, Springfield Moss	2-ft	
8717	20/28 H.P.	Alan Keef Ltd., Ross on Wye	2-ft	Dsm

W/n	Type	Location	Gauge	Status
8720	20/28 H.P.	Slate Mine Mus., Glyn Ceiriog, Clwyd	2-ft	
8723	20/28 H.P.	I.B.Jolly, nr. Mold, Clwyd	2-ft	Dsm
8727	20/28 H.P.	Andrew Johnston, Wedmore, Somerset	2-ft	
8729	20/28 H.P.	Lynton & Barnstaple Rly., Devon	2-ft	
8730	20/28 H.P.	Dover Transport Museum, Kent	2-ft	
8731	20/28 H.P.	Leighton Buzzard Rly., Beds.	2-ft	Dsm
8738	20/28 H.P.	Sinclair Horticultural, Auchencorth Moss	2-ft	
8739	20/28 H.P.	Butterley NGRA, Midland Rly. Centre	2-ft	
8745	20/28 H.P.	Museum of Army Transport, Beverley	2-ft	
8748	20/28 H.P.	Cadeby Lt. Rly., Cadeby, Leics.	2-ft	
8756	20/28 H.P.	H.Frampton-Jones, Surrey	2-ft	
8788	20/28 H.P.	Festiniog Rly.	2-ft	
8813	20/28 H.P.	Lime Kiln Wharf Rly., Stone, Staffs.	2-ft	
8820	20/28 H.P.	Lime Kiln Wharf Rly., Stone, Staffs.	2-ft	
8825	20/28 H.P.	Sinclair Horticultural, Bolton Fell, Cumbria	2-ft	
8826	20/28 H.P.	North Ings Farm Mus., Dorrington, Lincs.	2-ft	
8855	20/28 H.P.	Museum of Army Transport, Beverley	2-ft	
8856	20/28 H.P.	Exmoor Steam Rly., Bratton Fleming	2-ft	
8860	20/28 H.P.	Threlkeld Quarry Mus., Cumbria	2-ft	
8863	20/28 H.P.	Leadhills & Wanlockhead Rly.	2-ft	Dsm
8874	20/28 H.P.	Lincs. Coast Lt. Rly.	2-ft	
8875	20/28 H.P.	Alan Keef Ltd., Ross on Wye	2-ft	Dsm
8877	20/28 H.P.	Devon Railway Centre, Tiverton	2-ft	
8878	20/28 H.P.	Moseley Railway Trust	2-ft	
8882	20/28 H.P.	Alan Keef Ltd., Ross on Wye, Hereford	2-ft	
8884	20/28 H.P.	Leadhills & Wanlockhead Rly.	2-ft	Dsm
8885	20/28 H.P.	Levington Horticulture, Cumbria	2-ft	
8886	20/28 H.P.	Drillserve Ltd., Camborne, Cornwall	2-ft	
8887	20/28 H.P.	Old Kiln Rly., Tilford, Surrey	2-ft	
8905	20/28 H.P.	Levington Horticulture, Cumbria	2-ft	
8934	20/28 H.P.	C.Saxton, Redruth, Cornwall	2-ft	
8937	20/28 H.P.	Threlkeld Quarry Mus., Cumbria	2-ft	
8969	20/28 H.P.	Alan Keef Ltd, Ross on Wye	2-ft	
8979	20/28 H.P.	Embsay & Bolton Abbey Rly. NG group	2-ft	Dsm
8981	20/28 H.P.	Old Kiln Rly., Tilford, Surrey	2-ft	
8992	20/28 H.P.	West Lancs. Lt. Rly., Hesketh Bank, Lancs.	2-ft	
8994	20/28 H.P.	D.Webb, Tickhill, South Yorkshire	2-ft	
8995	20/28 H.P.	Alan Keef Ltd., Ross on Wye, Hereford	2-ft	
9104	20/26 H.P.	Moseley Railway Trust	2-ft	
9231	20/28 H.P.	Levington Horticulture, Cumbria	2-ft	
9264	20/28 H.P.	P.Walkinshaw, Eastgate, Deeping St. James	2-ft	
9381	20/28 H.P.	Alford Valley Rly., Grampian	2-ft	
9382	20/28 H.P.	Bromyard & Linton Rly., Herefordshire	2-ft	
9409	20/28 H.P.	Drusilla s Zoo Park, nr. Eastbourne	2-ft	

W/n	Type	Location	Gauge	Status
9547	20/28 H.P.	I.B.Jolly, nr. Mold, Clwyd	2-ft	
9655	20/28 H.P.	Stevington & Turvey Rly., Beds.	2-ft	
9676	20/28 H.P.	Bromyard & Linton Rly., Herefordshire	2-ft	
9677	20/28 H.P.	Bromyard & Linton Rly., Herefordshire	2-ft	
9709	20/28 H.P.	L&P Peat, Solway Moss, Cumbria	2-ft 6-in	
9710	20/28 H.P.	Alan Keef Ltd., Ross on Wye, Hereford	2-ft 6-in	
9711	20/28 H.P.	Ken Jackson, Eynsford, Kent	2-ft	
9774	20/28 H.P.	S.Smith, Herringfleet, Soffolk	2-ft	
9792	20/28 H.P.	Leadhills & Wanlockhead Rly.	2-ft	
9869	20/28 H.P.	Bygone Heritage Village, Fleggburgh	2-ft	
9976	20/28 H.P.	Cotswold Wildlife Park, Burford, Oxon.	2-ft	
9978	20/28 H.P.	B.Clarke, Bath, Somerset	2-ft	
9982	20/28 H.P.	D.Ritchie, Edinburgh	2-ft	
10161	32/42 H.P.	Amberley Museum, W. Sussex	2-ft 11-in	
10409	32/42 H.P.	Leighton Buzzard Rly., Beds.	2-ft	
11001	60S	Amberley Museum, W. Sussex	2-ft	
11003	60S	Leighton Buzzard Rly., Beds.	2-ft	
11102	60S	Welsh Highland Rly., Porthmadog	2-ft	
11111	60S	Vale of Teifi Rly., Llandyssul, Dyfed	2-ft	
11142	60S	Moseley Railway Trust	2-ft	
11143	60S	L.C.Pallot Trust, Jersey, Channel Islands	2-ft	S/O
11177	60S	Lynton & Barnstable Rly. Assoc., Devon	2-ft	
11218	60S	Astley Green Colliery Mus., Manchester	2-ft	
11223	60S	West Lancs. Lt. Rly., Hesketh Bank, Lancs.	2-ft	
11246	60S	Butterley NGRA, Midland Rly. Centre	2-ft	
11258	60S	West Lancs. Lt. Rly., Hesketh Bank, Lancs.	2-ft	
11264	60S	Nick Williams, Reading	2-ft	
11297	60S	Leighton Buzzard Rly., Beds.	2-ft	
11298	60S	Leighton Buzzard Rly., Beds.	2-ft	
20058	20/28 H.P.	Sinclair Horticultural, Bolton Fell, Cumbria	2-ft	
20070	20/28 H.P.	Peak Rail, Rowsley, Derbyshire	2-ft	
20073	20/28 H.P.	FMB Engineering Co., Hants.	2-ft	
20082	20/28 H.P.	Bromyard & Linton Rly., Hereford	2-ft	
20558	20/28 H.P.	I.B.Jolly, nr. Mold, Clwyd	2-ft	
21282	20/28 H.P.	Lea Bailey Mine, Newtown, Glos.	2-ft	
21505	20/28 H.P.	L&P Peat, Letham Moss, Airth, Central	2-ft	
21520	20/28 H.P.	L&P Peat, Letham Moss, Airth, Central	2-ft	
21579	20/28 H.P.	Festiniog Rly.	2-ft	
21615	20/28 H.P.	Leighton Buzzard Rly., Beds.	2-ft	
21619	20/28 H.P.	Alan Keef Ltd., Ross on Wye, Hereford	2-ft 6-in	
22021	40S	Isle of Man Rly. Soc., Isle of Man	2-ft 11-in	
22031	40S	Ashton Canal Carriers, Ashton-U-Lyne	2-ft	
22045	40S	Moseley Railway Trust	2-ft	
22119	40S	Festiniog Rly.	2-ft	Dsm

W/n	Type	Location	Gauge	Status
22128	40S	Sinclair Horticultural, Bolton Fell, Cumbria	2-ft	
22129	40S	Alan Keef Ltd., Ross on Wye, Hereford	2-ft	
22144	40S	Higham Ferrers Locomotives, Northants.	Metre	S/O
22154	40S	National Power, Dolgarrog Power Stn.	2-ft	
22209	40S	East Anglia Transport Mus., Lowestoft	2-ft	
22210	40S	Bressingham Steam Mus., Norfolk	1-ft 11-in	
22211	40S	East Anglia Transport Mus., Lowestoft	2-ft	
22221	40S	Alford Valley Rly., Grampian	2-ft	
22224	40S	Wicksteed Park, Kettering, NortHants.	2-ft	
22235	40S	David Jeffcot, Haslemere, Surrey	2-ft	
22236	40S	Drusillas Zoo Park, nr. Eastbourne	2-ft	
22237	40S	I.Hughs, Callender, Stirling	2-ft	
22238	40S	Sinclair Horticultural, Bolton Fell, Cumbria	2-ft	Dsm
22253	40S	Sinclair Horticultural, Springfield Moss	2-ft	
22258	40S	Corris Rly.	2-ft 3-in	
26007	10 H.P.	Micky Finn Rly., nr. Poole, Dorset	2-ft	
26014	12 H.P.	Treasure Train, Milkwall, nr. Coleford, Glos.	1-ft 3-in	
40S273	40S	Stoke Place Rly., Stoke Poges	2-ft	
40S280	40S	Isle of Man Rly.	3-ft	
40S302	40S	Scotts Co. (UK), Swinefleet, E. Yorks.	3-ft	
40S308	40S	Sinclair Horticultural, Cladance Moss	2-ft 6-in	
40S310	40S	Westonzoyland Eng Mus., Somerset	2-ft	
40S343	40S	L&P Peat, Letham Moss, Airth, Scotland	2-ft	Dsm
40S371	40S	L&P Peat, Solway Moss, Cumbria	2-ft 6-in	Dsm
40S383	40S	L&P Peat, Nutberry Moss, Dumfries	2-ft	
40S412	40S	Sinclair Horticultural, Bolton Fell, Cumbria	2-ft	Dsm
40SD501	40SD	Amerton Rly., Staffs.	2-ft	
40SD502	40SD	Severn Trent Water, Minworth	2-ft	
40SD503	40SD	Severn Trent Water, Minworth	2-ft	
40SD507	40SD	Scotts Co. (UK), Swinefleet, E. Yorks	3-ft	
40SD515	40SD	Severn Trent Water, Minworth	2-ft	
40SD516	40SD	Severn Trent Water, Minworth	2-ft	
40SP522	40SP	Almond Valley Heritage C tre, Lothian	2-ft 6-in	
40SD527	40SD	Scotts Co (UK), Hatfield Moor, S. Yorks.	3-ft	
40SD529	40SD	Butterley NGRA, Midland Rly. Centre	2-ft	
60S317	60S	Leighton Buzzard Rly., Beds.	2-ft	
60S318	60S	Blatchford Lt. Rly., Emborough, Somerset	2-ft	
60S333	60S	Welsh Highland Rly., Porthmadog	2-ft	
60S363	60S	Welsh Highland Rly., Porthmadog	2-ft	
60S364	60S	Butterley NGRA, Midland Rly. Centre	2-ft	
60S383	60S	L.C.Pallot Trust, Jersey, Channel Islands	2-ft	Dsm
60SD754	60SD	Embsay & Bolton Abbey Rly. NG Group	2-ft	
60SD755	60SD	Embsay & Bolton Abbey Rly. NG Group	2-ft	
102G038	G-Series	Bromyard & Linton Rly., Herefordshire	2-ft	

W/n	Type	Location	Gauge	Status
104G063	G-Series	Cadeby Lt. Rly., Cadeby, Leics.	2-ft	
105H006	H-Series	Devon Railway Centre, Tiverton	3-ft	
110U082	U-Series	Bo ness & Kinneil Rly., Scotland	3-ft	
115U094	U-Series	Sinclair Horticultural, Cladance Moss	2-ft 6-in	
121U117	U-Series	B. Harris scrapyard, Cwmbran	Metre	
101T018	T-Series	Leighton Buzzard Rly., Beds.	2-ft	
101T019	T-Series	Alan Keef Ltd., Ross on Wye	2-ft 6-in	Dsm
101T020	T-Series	Butterley NGRA, Midland Rly. Centre	2-ft	
101T023	T-Series	Talyllyn Rly.	2-ft 3-in	
-	20/36 H.P.	Yorkshire Engine Co (YEC L104)	2-ft	
-	20/28 H.P.	Yorkshire Engine Co (YEC L102)	2-ft	
?	20 H.P.	Stornoway Waterworks, Isle of Lewis	2-ft	Dsm
?	20/35 H.P.?	Great Bush Rly., Uckfield, Sussex	2-ft	

S/O: Steam Outline.
Dsm: Dismantled.

Notes:

Note 1: 2197, 3849 and 3995 are rebuilds of unidentified locos.
Note 2: 3663 is a rebuild of 435 undertaken in 1924.
Note 3: 3720 is a rebuild of 872 undertaken in 1925.
Note 4: 3797 is a rebuild of 1363 undertaken in 1926.
Note 5: 9231 was originally numbered 8665
Note 6: All locos of type 40S and 60S are referred to as such, although the earlier locos were known as 30 H.P. and 50 H.P. respectively when originally sold.
Note 7: All locos of 2-ft gauge prior to 1966 are believed to have been actually built to 60-cm gauge for greater versatility.

An unidentified early 40S is the subject of a late 1950s Motor Rail publicity shot at the Kempston Hardwick brickworks of Eastwood Flettons Ltd.